2nd Workshop on Structured Prediction for Natural Language Processing 2017

Copenhagen, Denmark
9 – 11 September 2017

ISBN: 978-1-5108-4751-4

Printed from e-media with permission by:

Curran Associates, Inc.
57 Morehouse Lane
Red Hook, NY 12571

Some format issues inherent in the e-media version may also appear in this print version.

Printed by Curran Associates, Inc. (2017)

For permission requests, please contact the Association for Computational Linguistics at the address below.

Association for Computational Linguistics
209 N. Eighth Street
Stroudsburg, Pennsylvania 18360

Phone: 1-570-476-8006
Fax: 1-570-476-0860

acl@aclweb.org

Additional copies of this publication are available from:

Curran Associates, Inc.
57 Morehouse Lane
Red Hook, NY 12571 USA
Phone: 845-758-0400
Fax: 845-758-2633
Email: curran@proceedings.com
Web: www.proceedings.com

EMNLP 2017

The Conference on Empirical Methods in Natural Language Processing

Proceedings of the 2nd Workshop on Structured Prediction for Natural Language Processing

September 9-11, 2017
Copenhagen, Denmark

Introduction

Welcome to the Second workshop on structured prediction for NLP!

Many prediction tasks in NLP involve assigning values to mutually dependent variables. For example, when designing a model to automatically perform linguistic analysis of a sentence or a document (e.g., parsing, semantic role labeling, or discourse analysis), it is crucial to model the correlations between labels. Many other NLP tasks, such as machine translation, textual entailment, and information extraction, can be also modeled as structured prediction problems.

In order to tackle such problems, various structured prediction approaches have been proposed, and their effectiveness has been demonstrated. Studying structured prediction is interesting from both NLP and machine learning (ML) perspectives. From the NLP perspective, syntax and semantics of the natural language are clearly structured and advances in this area will enable researchers to understand the linguistic structure of data. From the ML perspective, a large amount of available text data and complex linguistic structures bring challenges to the learning community. Designing expressive yet tractable models and studying efficient learning and inference algorithms become important issues.

Recently, there has been significant interest in non-standard structured prediction approaches that take advantage of non-linearity, latent components, and/or approximate inference in both the NLP and ML communities. Researchers have also been discussing the intersection between deep learning and structured prediction through the DeepStructure reading group. This workshop intends to bring together NLP and ML researchers working on diverse aspects of structured prediction and expose the participants to recent progress in this area.

This year we have eight papers covering various aspects of structured prediction, including neural networks, deep structured prediction, and imitation learning. We also invited four fantastic speakers. We hope you all enjoy the program!

Finally, we would like to thank all programming committee members, speakers, and authors. We are looking forward to seeing you in Copenhagen.

Organizers:

Kai-Wei Chang, UCLA
Ming-Wei Chang, Microsoft Research
Alexander Rush, Harvard University
Vivek Srikumar, University of Utah

Program Committee:

Amir Globerson, Tel Aviv University (Israel)
Alexander Schwing (UIUC)
Ivan Titov (University of Amsterdam)
Janardhan Rao Doppa (WSU)
Jason Eisner (JHU)
Karl Stratos (TTIC)
Kevin Gimpel (TTIC)
Luke Zettlemoyer (UW)
Matt Gormley (CMU)
Mohit Bansal (UNC)
Mo Yu (IBM)
Noah Smith (UW)
Parisa Kordjamshidi (Tulane University)
Raquel Urtasun (University of Toronto)
Roi Reichart (Technion)
Ofer Meshi (Google)
Scott Yih (Microsoft)
Shay Cohen (University of Edinburgh)
Shuohang Wang (Singapore Management University)
Waleed Ammar (AI2)
Yoav Artzi (Cornell)

Table of Contents

Conference Program

Thursday, September 7, 2016

9:00–10:30 Section 1

9:00–9:15 *Welcome*
Organizers

9:15–10:00 *Invited Talk*

10:00–10:30 *Dependency Parsing with Dilated Iterated Graph CNNs*
Emma Strubell and Andrew McCallum

10:30–11:00 *Coffee Break*

11:00–12:15 Section 2

11:00–11:45 *Invited Talk*

11:45–12:15 *Poster Madness*

12:15–14:00 *Lunch*

Thursday, September 7, 2016 (continued)

14:00–15:30 Section 3

14:00–14:45 *Poster Session*

Entity Identification as Multitasking
Karl Stratos

Towards Neural Machine Translation with Latent Tree Attention
James Bradbury and Richard Socher

Structured Prediction via Learning to Search under Bandit Feedback
Amr Sharaf and Hal Daumé III

Syntax Aware LSTM model for Semantic Role Labeling
Feng Qian, Lei Sha, Baobao Chang, LuChen Liu and Ming Zhang

Spatial Language Understanding with Multimodal Graphs using Declarative Learning based Programming
Parisa Kordjamshidi, Taher Rahgooy and Umar Manzoor

Boosting Information Extraction Systems with Character-level Neural Networks and Free Noisy Supervision
Philipp Meerkamp and Zhengyi Zhou

14:45–15:30 *Invited Talk*

15:30–16:00 *Coffee Break*

Thursday, September 7, 2016 (continued)

16:00–17:30 Section 4

16:00–16:45 Invited Talk

16:45–17:15 *Piecewise Latent Variables for Neural Variational Text Processing*
Iulian Vlad Serban, Alexander Ororbia II, Joelle Pineau and Aaron Courville

17:15–17:30 ***Closing***

Dependency Parsing with Dilated Iterated Graph CNNs

Emma Strubell **Andrew McCallum**
College of Information and Computer Sciences
University of Massachusetts Amherst
{strubell, mccallum}@cs.umass.edu

Abstract

Dependency parses are an effective way to inject linguistic knowledge into many downstream tasks, and many practitioners wish to efficiently parse sentences at scale. Recent advances in GPU hardware have enabled neural networks to achieve significant gains over the previous best models, these models still fail to leverage GPUs' capability for massive parallelism due to their requirement of sequential processing of the sentence. In response, we propose Dilated Iterated Graph Convolutional Neural Networks (DIG-CNNs) for graph-based dependency parsing, a graph convolutional architecture that allows for efficient end-to-end GPU parsing. In experiments on the English Penn TreeBank benchmark, we show that DIG-CNNs perform on par with some of the best neural network parsers.

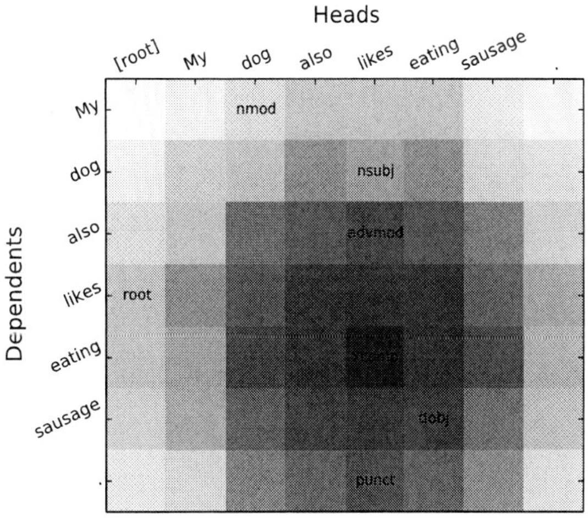

Figure 1: Receptive field for predicting the head-dependent relationship between *likes* and *eating*. Darker cell indicates more layers include that cell's representation. Heads and labels corresponding to gold tree are indicated.

1 Introduction

By vastly accelerating and parallelizing the core numeric operations for performing inference and computing gradients in neural networks, recent developments in GPU hardware have facilitated the emergence of deep neural networks as state-of-the-art models for many NLP tasks, such as syntactic dependency parsing. The best neural dependency parsers generally consist of two stages: First, they employ a recurrent neural network such as a bidirectional LSTM to encode each token in context; next, they compose these token representations into a parse tree. Transition based dependency parsers (Nivre, 2009; Chen and Manning, 2014; Andor et al., 2016) produce a well-formed tree by predicting and executing a series of shift-reduce actions, whereas graph-based parsers (McDonald et al., 2005; Kiperwasser and Goldberg, 2016; Dozat and Manning, 2017) generally employ attention to produce marginals over each possible edge in the graph, followed by a dynamic programming algorithm to find the most likely tree given those marginals.

Because of their dependency on sequential processing of the sentence, none of these architectures fully exploit the massive parallel processing capability that GPUs possess. If we wish to maximize GPU resources, graph-based dependency parsers are more desirable than their transition-based counterparts since attention over the edge-factored graph can be parallelized across the entire sentence, unlike the transition-based parser which must sequentially predict and perform each transition. By encoding token-level representations with

Proceedings of the 2nd Workshop on Structured Prediction for Natural Language Processing, pages 1–6
Copenhagen, Denmark, September 7–11, 2017.

an Iterated Dilated CNN (ID-CNN) (Strubell et al., 2017), we can also remove the sequential dependencies of the RNN layers. Unlike Strubell et al. (2017) who use 1-dimensional convolutions over the sentence to produce token representations, our network employs 2-dimensional convolutions over the adjacency matrix of the sentence's parse tree, modeling attention from the bottom up. By training with an objective that encourages our model to predict trees using only simple matrix operations, we additionally remove the additional computational cost of dynamic programming inference. Combining all of these ideas, we present Dilated Iterated Graph CNNs (DIG-CNNs): a combined convolutional neural network architecture and training objective for efficient, end-to-end GPU graph-based dependency parsing.

We demonstrate the efficacy of these models in experiments on English Penn TreeBank, in which our models perform similarly to the state-of-the-art.

2 Dilated Convolutions

Though common in other areas such as computer vision, 2-dimensional convolutions are rarely used in NLP since it is usually unclear how to process text as a 2-dimensional grid. However, 2-dimensional convolutional layers are a natural model for embedding the adjacency matrix of a sentence's parse.

A 2-dimensional convolutional neural network layer transforms each input element, in our case an edge in the dependency graph, as a linear function of the width r_w and height r_h window of surrounding input elements (other possible edges in the dependency graph). In this work we assume square convolutional windows: $r_h = r_w$.

Dilated convolutions perform the same operation, except rather than transforming directly adjacent inputs, the convolution is defined over a wider input window by skipping over δ inputs at a time, where δ is the dilation width. A dilated convolution of width 1 is equivalent to a simple convolution. Using the same number of parameters as a simple convolution with the same radius, the $\delta > 1$ dilated convolution incorporates broader context into the representation of a token than a simple convolution.

2.1 Iterated Dilated CNNs

Stacking many dilated CNN layers can easily incorporate information from a whole sentence. For example, with a radius of 1 and 4 layers of dilated convolutions, the effective input window size for each token is width 31, which exceeds the average sentence length (23) in the Penn TreeBank corpus. However, simply increasing the depth of the CNN can cause considerable over-fitting when data is sparse relative to the growth in model parameters. To address this, we employ Iterated Dilated CNNs (ID-CNNs) (Strubell et al., 2017), which instead apply the same small stack of dilated convolutions repeatedly, each time taking the result of the last stack as input to the current iteration. Applying the parameters recurrently in this way increases the size of the window of context incorporated into each token representation while allowing the model to generalize well. Their training objective additionally computes a loss for the output of each application, encouraging parameters that allow subsequent stacks to resolve dependency violations from their predecessors.

3 Dilated Iterated Graph CNNs

We describe how to extend ID-CNNs (Strubell et al., 2017) to 2-dimensional convolutions over the adjacency matrix of a sentence's parse tree, allowing us to model the parse tree through the whole network, incorporating evidence about nearby head-dependent relationships in every layer of the network, rather than modeling at the token level followed by a single layer of attention to produce head-dependent compatibilities between tokens. ID-CNNs allow us to efficiently incorporate evidence from the entire tree without sacrificing generalizability.

3.1 Model architecture

Let $x = [x_1, \ldots, x_T]$ be our input text[1] Let $y = [y_1, \ldots, y_T]$ be labels with domain size D for the edge between each token x_i and its head x_j. We predict the most likely y, given a conditional model $P(y|x)$ where the tags are conditionally independent given some features for x:

$$P(y|x) = \prod_{t=1}^{T} P(y_t|F(x)), \qquad (1)$$

[1]In practice, we include a dummy root token at the beginning of the sentence which serves as the head of the root. We do not predict a head for this dummy token.

The local conditional distributions of Eqn. (1) come from a straightforward extension of ID-CNNs (Strubell et al., 2017) to 2-dimensional convolutions. This network takes as input a sequence of T vectors $\mathbf{x_t}$, and outputs a $T \times T$ matrix of per-class scores $\mathbf{h_{ij}}$ for each pair of tokens in the sentence.

We denote the kth dilated convolutional layer of dilation width δ as $D_{\delta}^{(k)}$. The first layer in the network transforms the input to a graph by concatenating all pairs of vectors in the sequence $\mathbf{x_i}, \mathbf{x_j}$ and applying a 2-dimensional dilation-1 convolution $D_1^{(0)}$ to form an initial edge representation $\mathbf{c}_{\mathbf{ij}}^{(0)}$ for each token pair:

$$\mathbf{c_{ij}}^{(0)} = D_1^{(0)}[\mathbf{x_i}; \mathbf{x_j}] \quad (2)$$

We denote vector concatenation with $[\cdot;\cdot]$. Next, L_c layers of dilated convolutions of exponentially increasing dilation width are applied to $\mathbf{c_{ij}}^{(0)}$, folding in increasingly broader context into the embedded representation of $\mathbf{e_{ij}}$ at each layer. Let $r()$ denote the ReLU activation function (Glorot et al., 2011). Beginning with $\mathbf{c_t}^{(0)} = \mathbf{i_t}$ we define the stack of layers with the following recurrence:

$$\mathbf{c_{ij}}^{(k)} = r\left(D_{2^{L_c-1}}^{(k-1)} \mathbf{c_t}^{(k-1)}\right) \quad (3)$$

and add a final dilation-1 layer to the stack:

$$\mathbf{c_{ij}}^{(L_c+1)} = r\left(D_1^{(L_c)} \mathbf{c_t}^{(L_c)}\right) \quad (4)$$

We refer to this stack of dilated convolutions as a *block* $B(\cdot)$, which has output resolution equal to its input resolution. To incorporate even broader context without over-fitting, we avoid making B deeper, and instead iteratively apply B L_b times, introducing no extra parameters. Starting with $\mathbf{b_t}^{(1)} = B(\mathbf{i_t})$, we define the output of block m:

$$\mathbf{b_{ij}}^{(m)} = B\left(\mathbf{b_t}^{(m-1)}\right) \quad (5)$$

We apply a simple affine transformation W_o to this final representation to obtain label scores for each edge $\mathbf{e_{ij}}$:

$$\mathbf{h_{ij}}^{(L_b)} = W_o \mathbf{b_t}^{(L_b)} \quad (6)$$

We can obtain the most likely head (and its label) for each dependent by computing the argmax over all labels for all heads for each dependent:

$$\mathbf{h_t} = \arg\max_j \mathbf{h_{ij}}^{(L_b)} \quad (7)$$

3.2 Training

Our main focus is to apply the DIG-CNN as feature extraction for the conditional model described in Sec. 3.1, where tags are conditionally independent given deep features, since this will enable prediction that is parallelizable across all possible edges. Here, maximum likelihood training is straightforward because the likelihood decouples into the sum of the likelihoods of independent logistic regression problems for every edge, with natural parameters given by Eqn. (6):

$$\frac{1}{T}\sum_{t=1}^{T} \log P(y_t \mid \mathbf{h_t}) \quad (8)$$

We could also use the DIG-CNN as input features for an MST parser, where the partition function and its gradient are computed using Kirchhoffs Matrix-Tree Theorem (Tutte, 1984), but our aim is to approximate inference in a tree-structured graphical model using greedy inference and expressive features over the input in order to perform inference as efficiently as possible on a GPU.

To help bridge the gap between these two techniques, we use the training technique described in (Strubell et al., 2017). The tree-structured graphical model has preferable sample complexity and accuracy since prediction directly reasons in the space of structured outputs. Instead, we compile some of this reasoning in output space into DIG-CNN feature extraction. Instead of explicit reasoning over output labels during inference, we train the network such that each block is predictive of output labels. Subsequent blocks learn to correct dependency violations of their predecessors, refining the final sequence prediction.

To do so, we first define predictions of the model after each of the L_b applications of the block. Let $\mathbf{h_t}^{(m)}$ be the result of applying the matrix W_o from (6) to $\mathbf{b_t}^{(m)}$, the output of block m. We minimize the average of the losses for each application of the block:

$$\frac{1}{L_b}\sum_{k=1}^{L_b} \frac{1}{T}\sum_{t=1}^{T} \log P(y_t \mid \mathbf{h_t}^{(m)}). \quad (9)$$

By rewarding accurate predictions after each application of the block, we learn a model where later blocks are used to refine initial predictions. The loss also helps reduce the vanishing gradient problem (Hochreiter, 1998) for deep architectures.

We apply dropout (Srivastava et al., 2014) to the raw inputs $\mathbf{x_{ij}}$ and to each block's output $\mathbf{b_t}^{(m)}$ to help prevent overfitting.

4 Related work

Currently, the most accurate parser in terms of labeled and unlabeled attachment scores is the neural network graph-based dependency parser of Dozat and Manning (2017). Their parser builds token representations with a bidirectional LSTM over word embeddings, followed by head and dependent MLPs. Compatibility between heads and dependents is then scored using a biaffine model, and the highest scoring head for each dependent is selected.

Previously, (Chen and Manning, 2014) pioneered neural network paring with a transition-based dependency parser which used features from a fast feed-forward neural network over word, token and label embeddings. Many improved upon this work by increasing the size of the network and using a structured training objective (Weiss et al., 2015; Andor et al., 2016). (Kiperwasser and Goldberg, 2016) were the first to present a graph-based neural network parser, employing an MLP with bidirectional LSTM inputs to score arcs and labels. (Cheng et al., 2016) propose a similar network, except with additional forward and backward encoders to allow for conditioning on previous predictions. (Kuncoro et al., 2016) take a different approach, distilling a consensus of many LSTM-based transition-based parsers into one graph-based parser. (Ma and Hovy, 2017) employ a similar model, but add a CNN over characters as an additional word representation and perform structured training using the Matrix-Tree Theorem. Hashimoto et al. (2017) train a large network which performs many NLP tasks including part-of-speech tagging, chunking, graph-based parsing, and entailment, observing benefits from multitasking with these tasks.

Despite their success in the area of computer vision, in NLP convolutional neural networks have mainly been relegated to tasks such as sentence classification, where each input sequence is mapped to a single label (rather than a label for each token) Kim (2014); Kalchbrenner et al. (2014); Zhang et al. (2015); Toutanova et al. (2015). As described above, CNNs have also been used to encode token representations from embeddings of their characters, which similarly perform a pooling operation over characters. Lei et al. (2015) present a CNN variant where convolutions adaptively skip neighboring words. While the flexibility of this model is powerful, its adaptive behavior is not well-suited to GPU acceleration.

More recently, inspired by the success of deep dilated CNNs for image segmentation in computer vision (Yu and Koltun, 2016; Chen et al., 2015), convolutional neural networks have been employed as fast models for tagging, speech generation and machine translation. (van den Oord et al., 2016) use dilated CNNs to efficiently generate speech, and Kalchbrenner et al. (2016) describes an encoder-decoder model for machine translation which uses dilated CNNs over bytes in both the encoder and decoder. Strubell et al. (2017) first described the one-dimensional ID-CNN architecture which is the basis for this work, demonstrating its success as a fast and accurate NER tagger. Gehring et al. (2017) report state-of-the-art results and much faster training from using many CNN layers with gated activations as encoders and decoders for a sequence-to-sequence model. While our architecture is similar to the encoder architecture of these models, ours is differentiated by (1) being tailored to smaller-data regimes such as parsing via our iterated architecture and loss, and (2) employing two-dimensional convolutions to model the adjacency matrix of the parse tree. We are the first to our knowledge to use dilated convolutions for parsing, or to use two-dimensional dilated convolutions for NLP.

5 Experimental Results

5.1 Data and Evaluation

We train our parser on the English Penn TreeBank on the typical data split: training on sections 2–21, testing on section 23 and using section 22 for development. We convert constituency trees to dependencies using the Stanford dependency framework v3.5 (de Marneffe and Manning, 2008), and use part-of-speech tags from the Stanford left3words part-of-speech tagger. As is the norm for this dataset, our evaluation excludes punctuation. Hyperparameters that resulted in the best performance on the validation set were selected via grid search. A more detailed description of optimization and data pre-processing can be found in the Appendix.

Model	UAS	LAS
Kiperwasser and Goldberg (2016)	93.9	91.9
Cheng et al. (2016)	94.10	91.49
Kuncoro et al. (2016)	94.3	92.1
Hashimoto et al. (2017)	94.67	92.90
Ma and Hovy (2017)	94.9	93.0
Dozat and Manning (2017)	95.74	94.08
DIG-CNN	93.70	91.72
DIG-CNN + Eisner	94.03	92.00

Table 1: Labeled and unlabeled attachment scores of our model compared to state-of-the-art graph-based parsers

5.2 English PTB Results

We compare our models labeled and unlabeled attachment scores to the neural network graph-based dependency parsers described in Sec. 4. Without enforcing trees at test time, our model performs just under the LSTM-based parser of Kiperwasser and Goldberg (2016), and a few points lower than the state-of-the-art. When we post-process our model's outputs into trees, like all the other models in our table, our results increase to perform slightly above Kiperwasser and Goldberg (2016).

We believe our model's relatively poor performance compared to existing models is due to its limited incorporation of context from the entire sentence. While each bidirectional LSTM token representation observes all tokens in the sentence, our reported model observes a relatively small window, only 9 tokens. We hypothesize that this window is not sufficient for producing accurate parses. Still, we believe this is a promising architecture for graph-based parsing, and with further experimentation could meet or exceed the state-of-the-art while running faster by better leveraging GPU architecture.

6 Conclusion

We present DIG-CNNs, a fast, end-to-end convolutional architecture for graph-based dependency parsing. Future work will experiment with deeper CNN architectures which incorporate broader sentence context in order to increase accuracy without sacrificing speed.

Acknowledgments

We thank Patrick Verga and David Belanger for helpful discussions. This work was supported in part by the Center for Intelligent Information Retrieval, in part by DARPA under agreement number FA8750-13-2-0020, in part by Defense Advanced Research Agency (DARPA) contract number HR0011-15-2-0036, in part by the National Science Foundation (NSF) grant number DMR-1534431, and in part by the National Science Foundation (NSF) grant number IIS-1514053. The U.S. Government is authorized to reproduce and distribute reprints for Governmental purposes notwithstanding any copyright notation thereon. Any opinions, findings and conclusions or recommendations expressed in this material are those of the authors and do not necessarily reflect those of the sponsor.

References

Daniel Andor, Chris Alberti, David Weiss, Aliaksei Severyn, Alessandro Presta, Kuzman Ganchev, Slav Petrov, and Michael Collins. 2016. Globally normalized transition-based neural networks. In *Proceedings of the 54th Annual Meeting of the Association for Computational Linguistics*.

Danqi Chen and Christopher D. Manning. 2014. A fast and accurate dependency parser using neural networks. In *EMNLP*.

Liang-Chieh Chen, George Papandreou, Iasonas Kokkinos, Kevin Murphy, and Alan L. Yuille. 2015. Semantic image segmentation with deep convolutional nets and fully connected crfs. In *ICLR*.

Hao Cheng, Hao Fang, Xiaodong He, Jianfeng Gao, and Li Deng. 2016. Bi-directional attention with agreement for dependency parsing. In *EMNLP*.

Marie-Catherine de Marneffe and Christopher D. Manning. 2008. The stanford typed dependencies representation. In *COLING 2008 Workshop on Cross-framework and Cross-domain Parser Evaluation*.

Timothy Dozat and Christopher D. Manning. 2017. Deep biaffine attention for neural dependency parsing. In *ICLR*.

Jonas Gehring, Michael Auli, David Grangier, Denis Yarats, and Yann N. Dauphin. 2017. Convolutional sequence to sequence learning. *arXiv preprint: arXiv:1705.03122* .

Xavier Glorot, Antoine Bordes, and Yoshua Bengio. 2011. Deep sparse rectifier neural networks. In *AISTATS*.

Kazuma Hashimoto, Caiming Xiong, Yoshimasa Tsuruoka, and Richard Socher. 2017. A joint many-task model: Growing a neural network for multiple nlp tasks. *arXiv preprint: arXiv:1611.01587* .

Sepp Hochreiter. 1998. The vanishing gradient problem during learning recurrent neural nets and problem solutions. *International Journal of Uncertainty, Fuzziness and Knowledge-Based Systems* 6(02):107–116.

Nal Kalchbrenner, Lasse Espeholt, Karen Simonyan, Aaron van den Oord, Alex Graves, and Koray Kavukcuoglu. 2016. Neural machine translation in linear time. *arXiv preprint arXiv:1610.10099* .

Nal Kalchbrenner, Edward Grefenstette, and Phil Blunsom. 2014. A convolutional neural network for modelling sentences. In *Proceedings of the 52nd Annual Meeting of the Association for Computational Linguistics*.

Yoon Kim. 2014. Convolutional neural networks for sentence classification. In *EMNLP*.

Eliyahu Kiperwasser and Yoav Goldberg. 2016. Simple and accurate dependency parsing using bidirectional lstm feature representations. *Transactions of the Association for Computational Linguistics* 4:313–327.

Adhiguna Kuncoro, Miguel Ballesteros, Lingpeng Kong, Chris Dyer, and Noah A. Smith. 2016. Distilling an ensemble of greedy dependency parsers into one mst parser. In *EMNLP*.

Tao Lei, Regina Barzilay, and Tommi Jaakkola. 2015. Molding cnns for text: non-linear, non-consecutive convolutions. *Empirical Methods in Natural Language Processing* .

Xuezhe Ma and Eduard Hovy. 2017. Neural probabilistic model for non-projective mst parsing. *arXiv preprint: 1701.00874* .

Ryan McDonald, Fernando Pereira, Kiril Ribarov, and Jan Hajic. 2005. Non-projective dependency parsing using spanning tree algorithms. In *Proc. Human Language Technology Conf. and Conf. Empirical Methods Natural Language Process. (HLT/EMNLP)*. pages 523–530.

Joakim Nivre. 2009. Non-projective dependency parsing in expected linear time. In *Proceedings of the 47th Annual Meeting of the ACL and the 4th IJCNLP of the AFNLP*.

Nitish Srivastava, Geoffrey E Hinton, Alex Krizhevsky, Ilya Sutskever, and Ruslan Salakhutdinov. 2014. Dropout: a simple way to prevent neural networks from overfitting. *Journal of Machine Learning Research* 15(1):1929–1958.

Emma Strubell, Patrick Verga, David Belanger, and Andrew McCallum. 2017. Fast and accurate sequence labeling with iterated dilated convolutions. *arXiv preprint: arXiv:1702.02098* .

Kristina Toutanova, Danqi Chen, Patrick Pantel, Hoifung Poon, Pallavi Choudhury, and Michael Gamon. 2015. Representing text for joint embedding of text and knowledge bases. In *Proceedings of the 2015 Conference on Empirical Methods in Natural Language Processing*. Association for Computational Linguistics, pages 1499–1509.

William Thomas Tutte. 1984. *Graph theory*, volume 11. Addison-Wesley Menlo Park.

Aaron van den Oord, Sander Dieleman, Heiga Zen, Karen Simonyan, Oriol Vinyals, Alex Graves, Nal Kalchbrenner, Andrew Senior, and Koray Kavukcuoglu. 2016. Wavenet: A generative model for raw audio. *arXiv preprint arXiv:1609.03499* .

David Weiss, Chris Alberti, Michael Collins, and Slav Petrov. 2015. Structured training for neural network transition-based parsing. In *Annual Meeting of the Association for Computational Linguistics*.

Fisher Yu and Vladlen Koltun. 2016. Multi-scale context aggregation by dilated convolutions. In *International Conference on Learning Representations (ICLR)*.

Xiang Zhang, Junbo Zhao, and Yann LeCun. 2015. Character-level convolutional networks for text classification. In *Advances in Neural Information Processing Systems 28 (NIPS)*.

Entity Identification as Multitasking*

Karl Stratos
Toyota Technological Institute at Chicago
stratos@ttic.edu

Abstract

Standard approaches in entity identification hard-code boundary detection and type prediction into labels and perform Viterbi. This has two disadvantages: 1. the runtime complexity grows quadratically in the number of types, and 2. there is no natural segment-level representation. In this paper, we propose a neural architecture that addresses these disadvantages. We frame the problem as multitasking, separating boundary detection and type prediction but optimizing them jointly. Despite its simplicity, this architecture performs competitively with fully structured models such as BiLSTM-CRFs while scaling linearly in the number of types. Furthermore, by construction, the model induces type-disambiguating embeddings of predicted mentions.

1 Introduction

A popular convention in segmentation tasks such as named-entity recognition (NER) and chunking is the so-called "BIO"-label scheme. It hard-codes boundary detection and type prediction into labels using the indicators "B" (Beginning), "I" (Inside), and "O" (Outside). For instance, the sentence `Where is John Smith` is tagged as `Where/O is/O John/B-PER Smith/I-PER`. In this way, we can treat the problem as sequence labeling and apply standard structured models such as CRFs.

But this approach has certain disadvantages. First, the runtime complexity grows quadratically in the number of types (assuming exact decoding with first-order label dependency). We emphasize that the asymptotic runtime remains quadratic even if we heuristically prune previous labels based on the BIO scheme. This is not an issue when the number of types is small but quickly becomes problematic as the number grows. Second, there is no segment-level prediction: every prediction happens at the word-level. As a consequence, models do not induce representations corresponding to multi-word mentions, which can be useful for downstream tasks such as named-entity disambiguation (NED).

In this paper, we propose a neural architecture that addresses these disadvantages. Given a sentence, the model uses bidirectional LSTMs (BiLSTMs) to induce features and separately predicts:

1. Boundaries of mentions in the sentence.

2. Entity types of the boundaries.

Crucially, during training, the errors of these two predictions are minimized jointly.

One might suspect that the separation could degrade performance; neither prediction accounts for the correlation between entity types. But we find that this is not the case due to joint optimization. In fact, our model performs competitively with fully structured models such as BiLSTM-CRFs (Lample et al., 2016), implying that the model is able to capture the entity correlation indirectly by multitasking. On the other hand, the model scales linearly in the number of types and induces segment-level embeddings of predicted mentions that are type-disambiguating by construction.

*Part of the work was done while the author was at Bloomberg L. P.

Proceedings of the 2nd Workshop on Structured Prediction for Natural Language Processing, pages 7–11
Copenhagen, Denmark, September 7–11, 2017.

2 Related Work

Our work is directly inspired by Lample et al. (2016) who demonstrate that a simple neural architecture based on BiLSTMs achieves state-of-the-art performance on NER with no external features. They propose two models. The first makes structured prediction of NER labels with a CRF loss (LSTM-CRF) using the conventional BIO-label scheme. The second, which performs slightly worse, uses a shift-reduce framework mirroring tansition-based dependency parsing (Yamada and Matsumoto, 2003). While the latter also scales linearly in the number of types and produces embeddings of predicted mentions, our approach is quite different. We frame the problem as multitasking and do not need the stack/buffer data structure. Semi-Markov models (Kong et al., 2015; Sarawagi et al., 2004) explicitly incorporate the segment structure but are computationally intensive (quadratic in the sentence length).

Multitasking has been shown to be effective in numerous previous works (Collobert et al., 2011; Yang et al., 2016; Kiperwasser and Goldberg, 2016). This is especially true with neural networks which greatly simplify joint optimization across multiple objectives. Most of these works consider multitasking across different problems. In contrast, we decompose a single problem (NER) into two natural subtasks and perform them jointly. Particularly relevant in this regard is the parsing model of Kiperwasser and Goldberg (2016) which multitasks edge prediction and classification.

LSTMs (Hochreiter and Schmidhuber, 1997), and other variants of recurrent neural networks such as GRUs (Chung et al., 2014), have recently been wildly successful in various NLP tasks (Lample et al., 2016; Kiperwasser and Goldberg, 2016; Chung et al., 2014). Since there are many detailed descriptions of LSTMs available, we omit a precise definition. For our purposes, it is sufficient to treat an LSTM as a mapping $\phi : \mathbb{R}^d \times \mathbb{R}^{d'} \rightarrow \mathbb{R}^{d'}$ that takes an input vector x and a state vector h to output a new state vector $h' = \phi(x, h)$.

3 Model

Let $\mathcal{C}$ denote the set of character types, $\mathcal{W}$ the set of word types, and $\mathcal{E}$ the set of entity types. Let $\oplus$ denote the vector concatenation operation. Our model first constructs a network over a sentence closely following Lample et al. (2016); we describe it here for completeness. The model parameters Θ associated with this base network are

- Character embedding $e_c \in \mathbb{R}^{25}$ for $c \in \mathcal{C}$
- Character LSTMs $\phi_f^{\mathcal{C}}, \phi_b^{\mathcal{C}} : \mathbb{R}^{25} \times \mathbb{R}^{25} \rightarrow \mathbb{R}^{25}$
- Word embedding $e_w \in \mathbb{R}^{100}$ for $w \in \mathcal{W}$
- Word LSTMs $\phi_f^{\mathcal{W}}, \phi_b^{\mathcal{W}} : \mathbb{R}^{150} \times \mathbb{R}^{100} \rightarrow \mathbb{R}^{100}$

Let $w_1 \dots w_n \in \mathcal{W}$ denote a word sequence where word w_i has character $w_i(j) \in \mathcal{C}$ at position j. First, the model computes a character-sensitive word representation $v_i \in \mathbb{R}^{150}$ as

$$\begin{aligned} f_j^{\mathcal{C}} &= \phi_f^{\mathcal{C}}\left(e_{w_i(j)}, f_{j-1}^{\mathcal{C}}\right) & \forall j = 1 \dots |w_i| \\ b_j^{\mathcal{C}} &= \phi_b^{\mathcal{C}}\left(e_{w_i(j)}, b_{j+1}^{\mathcal{C}}\right) & \forall j = |w_i| \dots 1 \\ v_i &= f_{|w_i|}^{\mathcal{C}} \oplus b_1^{\mathcal{C}} \oplus e_{w_i} \end{aligned}$$

for each $i = 1 \dots n$.[1] Next, the model computes

$$\begin{aligned} f_i^{\mathcal{W}} &= \phi_f^{\mathcal{W}}\left(v_i, f_{i-1}^{\mathcal{W}}\right) & \forall i = 1 \dots n \\ b_i^{\mathcal{W}} &= \phi_b^{\mathcal{W}}\left(v_i, b_{i+1}^{\mathcal{W}}\right) & \forall i = n \dots 1 \end{aligned}$$

and induces a character- and context-sensitive word representation $h_i \in \mathbb{R}^{200}$ as

$$h_i = f_i^{\mathcal{W}} \oplus b_i^{\mathcal{W}} \tag{1}$$

for each $i = 1 \dots n$. These vectors are used to define the boundary detection loss and the type classification loss described below.

Boundary detection loss We frame boundary detection as predicting BIO tags without types. A natural approach is to optimize the conditional probability of the correct tags $y_1 \dots y_n \in \{\texttt{B}, \texttt{I}, \texttt{O}\}$:

$$p(y_1 \dots y_n | h_1 \dots h_n) \propto \exp\left(\sum_{i=1}^{n} T_{y_{i-1}, y_i} \times g_{y_i}(h_i)\right) \tag{2}$$

where $g : \mathbb{R}^{200} \rightarrow \mathbb{R}^3$ is a function that adjusts the length of the LSTM output to the number of targets. We use a feedforward network $g(h) = W^2 \text{relu}(W^1 h + b^1) + b^2$. We write Θ_1 to refer to $T \in \mathbb{R}^{3 \times 3}$ and the parameters in g. The boundary detection loss is given by the negative log likelihood:

$$L_1(\Theta, \Theta_1) = -\sum_l \log p\left(y^{(l)} | h^{(l)}\right)$$

[1] For simplicity, we assume some random initial state vectors such as $f_0^{\mathcal{C}}$ and $b_{|w_i|+1}^{\mathcal{C}}$ when we describe LSTMs.

where l iterates over tagged sentences in the data.

The global normalizer for (2) can be computed using dynamic programming; see Collobert et al. (2011). Note that the runtime complexity of boundary detection is constant despite dynamic programming since the number of tags is fixed (three).

Type classification loss Given a mention boundary $1 \leq s \leq t \leq n$, we predict its type using (1) as follows. We introduce an additional pair of LSTMs $\phi_f^{\mathcal{E}}, \phi_b^{\mathcal{E}} : \mathbb{R}^{200} \times \mathbb{R}^{200} \rightarrow \mathbb{R}^{200}$ and compute a corresponding mention representation $\mu \in \mathbb{R}^{|\mathcal{E}|}$ as

$$\begin{aligned} f_j^{\mathcal{E}} &= \phi_f^{\mathcal{E}}\left(h_j, f_{j-1}^{\mathcal{E}}\right) & \forall j = s \dots t \\ b_j^{\mathcal{E}} &= \phi_b^{\mathcal{E}}\left(h_j, b_{j+1}^{\mathcal{E}}\right) & \forall j = t \dots s \\ \mu &= q\left(f_t^{\mathcal{E}} \oplus b_s^{\mathcal{E}}\right) & \quad (3) \end{aligned}$$

where $q : \mathbb{R}^{400} \rightarrow \mathbb{R}^{|\mathcal{E}|}$ is again a feedforward network that adjusts the vector length to $|\mathcal{E}|$.[2] We write Θ_2 to refer to the parameters in $\phi_f^{\mathcal{E}}, \phi_b^{\mathcal{E}}, q$. Now we can optimize the conditional probability of the correct type τ:

$$p(\tau | h_s \dots h_t) \propto \exp\left(\mu_\tau\right) \quad (4)$$

The type classification loss is given by the negative log likelihood:

$$L_2\left(\Theta, \Theta_2\right) = -\sum_l \log p\left(\tau^{(l)} | h_s^{(l)} \dots h_t^{(l)}\right)$$

where l iterates over typed mentions in the data.

Joint loss The final training objective is to minimize the sum of the boundary detection loss and the type classification loss:

$$L(\Theta, \Theta_1, \Theta_2) = L_1\left(\Theta, \Theta_1\right) + L_2\left(\Theta, \Theta_2\right) \quad (5)$$

In stochastic gradient descent (SGD), this amounts to computing the tagging loss l_1 and the classification loss l_2 (summed over all mentions) at each annotated sentence, and then taking a gradient step on $l_1 + l_2$. Observe that the base network Θ is optimized to handle both tasks. During training, we use gold boundaries and types to optimize $L_2\left(\Theta, \Theta_2\right)$. At test time, we predict boundaries from the tagging layer (2) and classify them using the classification layer (4).

[2] Clearly, one can consider different networks over the boundary, for instance simple bag-of-words or convolutional neural networks. We leave the exploration as future work.

CoNLL 2003 (4 types)	F1	# words/sec
BiLSTM-CRF	90.22	3889
Mention2Vec	90.90	4825
OntoNotes (18 types)	**F1**	**# words/sec**
BiLSTM-CRF	90.77	495
Mention2Vec	89.37	4949

Table 1: Test F1 scores on CoNLL 2003 and OntoNotes newswire portion.

Model	F1
McCallum and Li (2003)	84.04
Collobert et al. (2011)	89.59
Lample et al. (2016)–Greedy	89.15
Lample et al. (2016)–Stack	90.33
Lample et al. (2016)–CRF	90.94
Mention2Vec	90.90

Table 2: Test F1 scores on CoNLL 2003.

4 Experiments

Data We use two NER datasets: CoNLL 2003 which has four entity types PER, LOC, ORG and MISC (Tjong Kim Sang and De Meulder, 2003), and the newswire portion of OntoNotes Release 5.0 which has 18 entity types (Weischedel et al., 2013).

Implementation and baseline We denote our model Mention2Vec and implement it using the DyNet library.[3] We use the same pre-trained word embeddings in Lample et al. (2016). We use the Adam optimizer (Kingma and Ba, 2014) and apply dropout at all LSTM layers (Hinton et al., 2012). We perform minimal tuning over development data. Specifically, we perform a 5×5 grid search over learning rates $0.0001 \dots 0.0005$ and dropout rates $0.1 \dots 0.5$ and choose the configuration that gives the best performance on the dev set.

We also re-implement the BiLSTM-CRF model of Lample et al. (2016); this is equivalent to optimizing just $L_1(\Theta, \Theta_1)$ but using typed BIO tags. Lample et al. (2016) use different details in optimization (SGD with gradient clipping), data preprocessing (replacing every digit with a zero), and the dropout scheme (droptout at BiLSTM input (1)). As a result, our re-implementation is not directly comparable and obtains different (slightly lower) results. But we emphasize that the main goal of this paper is to demonstrate the utility the

[3] https://github.com/karlstratos/mention2vec

PER	In another letter dated January 1865, a well-to-do Washington matron wrote to **Lincoln** to plead for ...
	Chang and **Washington** were the only men's seeds in action on a day that saw two seeded women's ... "Just one of those things, I was just trying to make contact," said **Bragg**. **Washington**'s win was not comfortable, either.
LOC	Lauck, from **Lincoln**, Nebraska, yelled a tirade of abuse at the court after his conviction for inciting ...
	... warring factions, with the PUK aming to break through to KDP's headquarters in **Saladhuddin**. ... is not expected to travel to the **West Bank** before Monday," Nabil Abu Rdainah told Reuters. ... off a bus near his family home in the village of **Donje Ljupce** in the municipality of Podujevo.
ORG	English division three - Swansea v **Lincoln**.
	SOCCER - OUT-OF-SORTS **NEWCASTLE** CRASH 2 1 AT HOME. Moura, who appeared to have elbowed Cyprien in the final minutes of the 3 0 win by **Neuchatel**, was ... In Sofia: Leviski Sofia (Bulgaria) 1 **Olimpija** (Slovenia) 0
WORK_OF_ART	... Bond novels, and "**Treasure Island**," produced by Charlton Heston who also stars in the movie.
	... probably started in 1962 with the publication of Rachel Carson's book "**Silent Spring**." ... Victoria Petrovich) spout philosophic bon mots with the self-concious rat-a-tat pacing of "**Laugh In**." Dennis Farney's Oct. 13 page - one article "**River of Despair**," about the poverty along the ...
GPE	... from a naval station at **Treasure Island** near the Bay Bridge to San Francisco to help fight fires.
	... lived in an expensive home on **Lido Isle**, an island in Newport's harbor, according to investigators. ... Doris Moreno, 37, of **Bell Gardens**; and Ana L. Azucena, 27, of Huntington Park. One group of middle-aged manufacturing men from the company's **Zama** plant outside Tokyo was ...
ORG	... initiative will spur members of **the General Agreement on Tariffs and Trade** to reach ...
	... question of Taiwan's membership in **the General Agreement on Tariffs and Trade** should ... "He doesn't know himself," Kathy Stanwick of **the Abortion Rights League** says of ... ... administrative costs, management and research, **the Office of Technology Assessment** just reported.

Table 3: Nearest neighbors of detected mentions in CoNLL 2003 and OntoNotes using (3).

proposed approach rather than obtaining a new state-of-the-art result on NER.

4.1 NER Performance

Table 1 compares the NER performance and decoding speed between BiLSTM-CRF and Mention2Vec. The F1 scores are obtained on test data. The speed is measured by the average number of words decoded per second.

On CoNLL 2003 in which the number of types is small, our model achieves 90.50 compared to 90.22 of BiLSTM-CRF with minor speed improvement. This shows that despite the separation between boundary detection and type classification, we can achieve good performance through joint optimization. On OntoNotes in which the number of types is much larger, our model still performs well with an F1 score of 89.37 but is behind BiLSTM-CRF which achieves 90.77. We suspect that this is due to strong correlation between mention types that fully structured models can exploit more effectively. However, our model is also an order of magnitude faster: 4949 compared to 495 words/second.

Finally, Table 2 compares our model with other works in the literature on CoNLL 2003. McCallum and Li (2003) use CRFs with manually crafted features; Collobert et al. (2011) use convolutional neural networks; Lample et al. (2016) use BiLSTMs in a greedy tagger (Greedy), a stack-based model (Stack), and a global tagger using a CRF output layer (CRF). Mention2Vec performs competitively.

4.2 Mention Embeddings

Table 3 shows nearest neighbors of detected mentions using the mention representations μ in (3). Since μ_τ represents the score of type τ, the mention embeddings are clustered by entity types *by construction*. The model induces completely different representations even when the mention has the same lexical form. For instance, based on its context `Lincoln` receives a person, location, or organization representation; `Treasure Island` receives a book or location representation. The model also learns representations for long multi-word expressions such as `the General Agreement on Tariffs and Trade`.

5 Conclusion

We have presented a neural architecture for entity identification that multitasks boundary detection and type classification. Joint optimization enables the base BiLSTM network to capture the correlation between entities indirectly via multitasking. As a result, the model is competitive with fully structured models such as BiLSTM-CRFs on CoNLL 2003 while being more scalable and also inducing context-sensitive mention embeddings clustered by entity types. There are many interesting future directions, such as applying this framework to NED in which type classification is much more fine-grained and finding a better method for optimizing the multitasking objective (e.g., instead of using gold boundaries for training, dynamically use predicted boundaries in a reinforcement learning framework).

Acknowledgments

The author would like to thank Linpeng Kong for his consistent help with DyNet and Miguel Ballesteros for pre-trained word embeddings.

References

Junyoung Chung, Caglar Gulcehre, KyungHyun Cho, and Yoshua Bengio. 2014. Empirical evaluation of gated recurrent neural networks on sequence modeling. In *NIPS Deep Learning Workshop*.

Ronan Collobert, Jason Weston, Léon Bottou, Michael Karlen, Koray Kavukcuoglu, and Pavel Kuksa. 2011. Natural language processing (almost) from scratch. *The Journal of Machine Learning Research* 12:2493–2537.

Geoffrey E Hinton, Nitish Srivastava, Alex Krizhevsky, Ilya Sutskever, and Ruslan R Salakhutdinov. 2012. Improving neural networks by preventing co-adaptation of feature detectors. *arXiv preprint arXiv:1207.0580* .

Sepp Hochreiter and Jürgen Schmidhuber. 1997. Long short-term memory. *Neural computation* 9(8):1735–1780.

Diederik Kingma and Jimmy Ba. 2014. Adam: A method for stochastic optimization. *arXiv preprint arXiv:1412.6980* .

Eliyahu Kiperwasser and Yoav Goldberg. 2016. Simple and accurate dependency parsing using bidirectional lstm feature representations. *Transactions of the Association for Computational Linguistics* 4:313–327.

Lingpeng Kong, Chris Dyer, and Noah A Smith. 2015. Segmental recurrent neural networks. *arXiv preprint arXiv:1511.06018* .

Guillaume Lample, Miguel Ballesteros, Sandeep Subramanian, Kazuya Kawakami, and Chris Dyer. 2016. Neural architectures for named entity recognition. In *Proceedings of NAACL*.

Andrew McCallum and Wei Li. 2003. Early results for named entity recognition with conditional random fields, feature induction and web-enhanced lexicons. In *Proceedings of the seventh conference on Natural language learning at HLT-NAACL 2003-Volume 4*. Association for Computational Linguistics, pages 188–191.

Barbara Plank. 2016. Keystroke dynamics as signal for shallow syntactic parsing. In *Proceedings of COLING*.

Barbara Plank, Anders Søgaard, and Yoav Goldberg. 2016. Multilingual part-of-speech tagging with bidirectional long short-term memory models and auxiliary loss. In *Proceedings of ACL*.

Sunita Sarawagi, William W Cohen, et al. 2004. Semi-markov conditional random fields for information extraction. In *NIPs*. volume 17, pages 1185–1192.

Erik F Tjong Kim Sang and Fien De Meulder. 2003. Introduction to the conll-2003 shared task: Language-independent named entity recognition. In *Proceedings of the seventh conference on Natural language learning at HLT-NAACL 2003-Volume 4*. Association for Computational Linguistics, pages 142–147.

Ralph Weischedel, Martha Palmer, Mitchell Marcus, Eduard Hovy, Sameer Pradhan, Lance Ramshaw, Nianwen Xue, Ann Taylor, Jeff Kaufman, Michelle Franchini, et al. 2013. Ontonotes release 5.0 ldc2013t19. *Linguistic Data Consortium, Philadelphia, PA* .

Hiroyasu Yamada and Yuji Matsumoto. 2003. Statistical dependency analysis with support vector machines. In *Proceedings of IWPT*. volume 3, pages 195–206.

Zhilin Yang, Ruslan Salakhutdinov, and William Cohen. 2016. Multi-task cross-lingual sequence tagging from scratch. *arXiv preprint arXiv:1603.06270* .

Towards Neural Machine Translation with Latent Tree Attention

James Bradbury and **Richard Socher**
james.bradbury@salesforce.com
rsocher@salesforce.com

Abstract

Building models that take advantage of the hierarchical structure of language without *a priori* annotation is a longstanding goal in natural language processing. We introduce such a model for the task of machine translation, pairing a recurrent neural network grammar encoder with a novel attentional RNNG decoder and applying policy gradient reinforcement learning to induce unsupervised tree structures on both the source and target. When trained on character-level datasets with no explicit segmentation or parse annotation, the model learns a plausible segmentation and shallow parse, obtaining performance close to an attentional baseline.

1 Introduction

Many efforts to exploit linguistic hierarchy in NLP tasks make use of the output of a self-contained parser system trained from a human-annotated treebank (Huang et al., 2006). An alternative approach aims to jointly learn the task at hand and relevant aspects of linguistic hierarchy, inducing from an unannotated training dataset parse trees that may or may not correspond to treebank annotation practices (Wu, 1997; Chiang, 2005).

Most deep learning models for NLP that aim to make use of linguistic hierarchy integrate an external parser, either to prescribe the recursive structure of the neural network (Pollack, 1990; Goller and Küchler, 1996; Socher et al., 2013) or to provide a supervision signal or training data for a network that predicts its own structure (Socher et al., 2010; Bowman et al., 2016; Dyer et al., 2016b). But some recently described neural network models take the second approach and treat hierarchical structure as a latent variable, applying inference over graph-based conditional random fields (Kim et al., 2017), the straight-through estimator (Chung et al., 2017), or policy gradient reinforcement learning (Yogatama et al., 2017) to work around the inapplicability of gradient-based learning to problems with discrete latent states.

For the task of machine translation, syntactically-informed models have shown promise both inside and outside the deep learning context, with hierarchical phrase-based models frequently outperforming traditional ones (Chiang, 2005) and neural MT models augmented with morphosyntactic input features (Sennrich and Haddow, 2016; Nadejde et al., 2017), a tree-structured encoder (Eriguchi et al., 2016; Hashimoto and Tsuruoka, 2017), and a jointly trained parser (Eriguchi et al., 2017) each outperforming purely-sequential baselines.

Drawing on many of these precedents, we introduce an attentional neural machine translation model whose encoder and decoder components are both tree-structured neural networks that predict their own constituency structure as they consume or emit text. The encoder and decoder networks are variants of the RNNG model introduced by Dyer et al. (2016b), allowing tree structures of unconstrained arity, while text is ingested at the character level, allowing the model to discover and make use of structure within words.

The parsing decisions of the encoder and decoder RNNGs are parameterized by a stochastic policy trained using a weighted sum of two objectives: a language model loss term that rewards predicting the next character with high likelihood, and a tree attention term that rewards one-to-one attentional correspondence between constituents in the encoder and decoder.

We evaluate this model on the German-English language pair of the `flickr30k` dataset, where it obtains similar performance to a strong character-

Proceedings of the 2nd Workshop on Structured Prediction for Natural Language Processing, pages 12–16
Copenhagen, Denmark, September 7–11, 2017.

level baseline. Analysis of the latent trees produced by the encoder and decoder shows that the model learns a reasonable segmentation and shallow parse, and most phrase-level constituents constructed while ingesting the German input sentence correspond meaningfully to constituents built while generating the English output.

2 Model

2.1 Encoder/Decoder Architecture

The model consists of a coupled encoder and decoder, where the encoder is a modified stack-only recurrent neural network grammar (Kuncoro et al., 2017) and the decoder is a stack-only RNNG augmented with constituent-level attention. An RNNG is a top-down transition-based model that jointly builds a sentence representation and parse tree, representing the parser state with a StackLSTM and using a bidirectional LSTM as a constituent composition function. Our implementation is detailed in Figure 1, and differs from Dyer et al. (2016b) in that it lacks separate new-nonterminal tokens for different phrase types, and thus does not include the phrase type as an input to the composition function. Instead, the values of $\mathbf{x}_i$ for the encoder are fixed to a constant $\mathbf{x}^{\text{enc}}$ while the values of $\mathbf{x}_j$ for the decoder are determined through an attention procedure (Section 2.2).

As originally described, the RNNG predicts parser transitions using a one-layer $\tanh$ perceptron with three concatenated inputs: the last state of a unidirectional LSTM over the stack contents ($\mathbf{s}$), the last state of a unidirectional LSTM over the reversed buffer of unparsed tokens ($\mathbf{b}$), and the result of an LSTM over the past transitions ($\mathbf{a}$). All three of these states can be computed with at most one LSTM step per parser transition using the StackLSTM algorithm (Dyer et al., 2016a). But such a baseline RNNG is actually outperformed by one which conditions the parser transitions only on the stack representation (Kuncoro et al., 2017). Restricting our model to this stack-only case allows both the encoder and decoder to be supervised using a language model loss, while allowing the model access to $\mathbf{b}$ would give it a trivial way to predict the next character and obtain zero loss.

2.2 Attention

With the exception of the attention mechanism, the encoder and decoder are identical. While the encoder uses a single token to represent a new nonterminal, the decoder represents a new nonterminal on the stack as a sum weighted by *structural attention* of the *phrase representations* of all nonterminal tree nodes produced by the encoder. In particular, we use the normalized dot products between the decoder stack representation $\mathbf{s}_j^{\text{dec}}$ and the stack representation at each encoder node $\mathbf{s}_{\text{enc}}^i$ (that is, the hidden state of the StackLSTM up to and including $\mathbf{x}_j^{\text{enc}}$ but not $\mathbf{h}_j^{\text{enc}}$) as coefficients in a weighted sum of the phrase embeddings $\mathbf{h}_{\text{enc}}^i$ corresponding to the encoder nodes:

$$\begin{aligned} \alpha_{ij} &= \operatorname*{softmax}_{\text{all } i}(\mathbf{s}_i^{\text{enc}} \cdot \mathbf{s}_j^{\text{dec}}) \\ \mathbf{x}_j^{\text{dec}} &= \sum_i \alpha_{ij} \mathbf{h}_i^{\text{enc}}. \end{aligned} \tag{1}$$

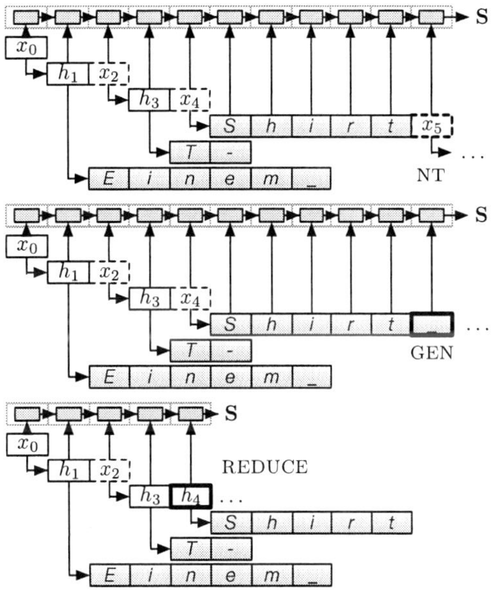

Figure 1: At a given timestep during either encoding or decoding there are three possible transitions (although one or more may be forbidden): begin a new nonterminal constituent (NT), predict and ingest a terminal (GEN), or end the current nonterminal (REDUCE). If the chosen transition is NT, the RNNG adds a new-nonterminal token $\mathbf{x}_{i+1}$ to the active constituent and begins a new nonterminal constituent (**1a**). If the transition is GEN, the RNNG predicts the next token (Section 2.3) and adds the ground-truth next token $\mathbf{e}$ from the context buffer at the cursor location (**1b**). If the transition is REDUCE, the contents of the active nonterminal are passed to the composition function, the new-nonterminal token $\mathbf{x}_i$ is replaced with the result of the composition $\mathbf{h}_i$, and the StackLSTM rolls back to the previously active constituent (**1c**). In all three cases, the StackLSTM then advances one step with the newly added token as input ($\mathbf{x}_{i+1}$, $\mathbf{e}$, or $\mathbf{h}_i$).

Since the dot products between encoder and decoder stack representations are a measure of structural similarity between the (left context of) the current decoder state and the encoder state. Within a particular decoder nonterminal, the model reduces to ordinary sequence-to-sequence transduction. Starting from the encoder's representation of the corresponding nonterminal or a weighted combination of such representations, the decoder will emit a translated sequence of child constituents (both nonterminal and terminal) one by one—applying attention only when emitting nonterminal children.

2.3 Training

We formulate our model as a stochastic computation graph (Schulman et al., 2015), leading to a training paradigm that combines backpropagation (which provides the exact gradient through deterministic nodes) and vanilla policy gradient (which provides a Monte Carlo estimator for the gradient through stochastic nodes).

There are several kinds of training signals in our model. First, when the encoder or decoder chooses the GEN action it passes the current stack state s through a one-layer softmax perceptron, giving the probability that the next token is each of the characters in the vocabulary. The language model loss $\mathcal{L}_k$ for each generated token is the negative log probability assigned to the ground-truth next token. The other differentiable training signal is the coverage loss $\mathcal{L}_c$, which is a measure of how much the attention weights diverge from the ideal of a one-to-one mapping. This penalty is computed as a sum of three MSE terms:

$$\begin{aligned}\mathcal{L}_c = &\operatorname*{mean}_{\text{all } i}(1 - \sum_{\text{all } j} \alpha_{ij})^2 \\ &+ \operatorname*{mean}_{\text{all } i}(1 - \max_{\text{all } j} \alpha_{ij})^2 \\ &+ \operatorname*{mean}_{\text{all } j}(1 - \max_{\text{all } i} \alpha_{ij})^2\end{aligned} \tag{2}$$

Backpropagation using the differentiable losses affects only the weights of the output softmax perceptron. The overall loss function for these weights is a weighted sum of all $\mathcal{L}_k$ terms and $\mathcal{L}_c$:

$$\mathcal{L} = 100\mathcal{L}_c + 10 \sum_{\text{all } k} \mathcal{L}_k \tag{3}$$

There are additionally nondifferentiable rewards r that bias the model towards or away from certain kinds of tree structures. Here, negative numbers correspond to penalties. We assign a tree reward of -1 when the model predicts a REDUCE with only one child constituent (REDUCE with zero child constituents is forbidden) or predicts two REDUCE or NT transitions in a row. This biases the model against unary branching and reduces its likelihood of producing an exclusively left- or right-branching tree structure. In addition, for all constituents except the root, we assign a tree reward based on the size and type of its children. If n and t are the number of nonterminal and terminal children, this reward is $4t$ if all children are terminal and $9\sqrt{n}$ otherwise. A reward structure like this biases the model against freely mixing terminals and nonterminals within the same constituent and provides incentive to build substantial tree structures early on in training so the model doesn't get stuck in trivial local minima.

Within both the encoder and decoder, each stochastic action node has a corresponding tree reward r_k if the action was REDUCE (otherwise zero) and a corresponding language model loss $\mathcal{L}_k$ if the action was GEN (otherwise zero). We subtract an exponential moving average baseline from each tree reward and additional exponential moving average baselines—computed independently for each character z in the vocabulary, because we want to reduce the effect of character frequency—from the language model losses. If $\text{GEN}(k)$ is the number of GEN transitions among actions one through k, and γ is a decay constant, the final reward $\mathcal{R}_k^m$ for action k with $m \in \{\text{enc}, \text{dec}\}$ is:

$$\begin{aligned}\hat{r}_k &= r_k - r_{\text{baseline}} \\ \hat{\mathcal{L}}_k &= \mathcal{L}_k - \mathcal{L}_{\text{baseline}}(z_k) \\ \hat{\mathcal{R}}_k &= \sum_{\kappa=k}^{K_m} \gamma^{\text{GEN}(\kappa)-\text{GEN}(k)} (\hat{r}_\kappa - \hat{\mathcal{L}}_\kappa^m) \\ \mathcal{R}_k^{\text{enc}} &= \hat{\mathcal{R}}_k - \mathcal{L}_c - (m = \text{enc}) \sum_{\kappa=1}^{K_{\text{dec}}} \mathcal{L}_k^{\text{dec}}.\end{aligned} \tag{4}$$

These rewards define the gradient that each stochastic node (with normalized action probabilities p_k^a and chosen action a_k) produces during backpropagation according to the standard multinomial score function estimator (REINFORCE):

$$\nabla_\theta p_k^a = \operatorname*{mean}_{a_k = a} \mathcal{R}_k \nabla_\theta \log p_k^{a_k} = \operatorname*{mean}_{a_k = a} \frac{-\mathcal{R}_k}{p_k^{a_k}} \tag{5}$$

3 Results

We evaluated our model on the German-English language pair of the `flickr30k` data, the tex-

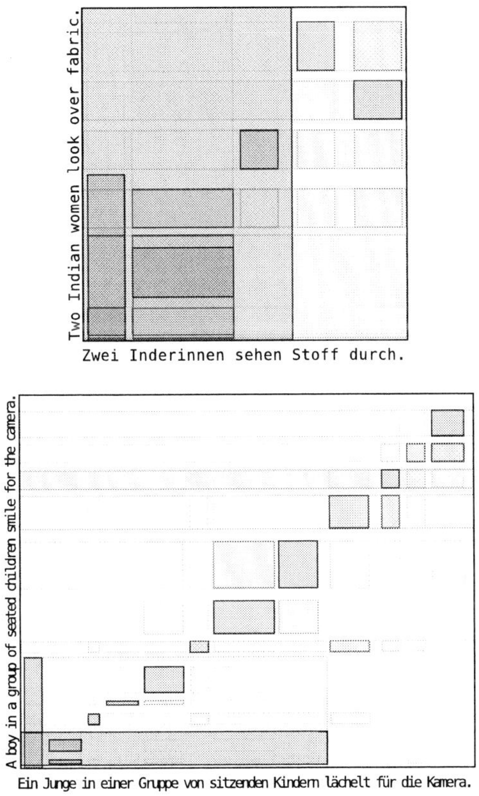

Figure 2: Attention visualizations for two sentences from the development set. Attention between two constituents is represented by a shaded rectangle whose projections on the x and y axes cover the encoder and decoder constituents respectively.

tual component of the WMT Multimodal Translation shared task (Specia et al., 2016). An attentional sequence-to-sequence model with two layers and 384 hidden units from the OpenNMT project (Klein et al., 2017) was run at the character level as a baseline, obtaining 32.0 test BLEU with greedy inference. Our model with the same hidden size and greedy inference achieves test BLEU of 28.5 after removing repeated bigrams.

We implemented the model in PyTorch, benefiting from its strong support for dynamic and stochastic computation graphs, and trained with batch size 10 and the Adam optimizer (Kingma and Ba, 2015) with early stopping after 12 epochs. Character embeddings and the encoder's $\mathbf{x}^{\text{enc}}$ embedding were initialized to random 384-dimensional vectors. The value of γ and the decay constant for the baselines' exponential moving average were both set to 0.95. A random selection of translations is included in the supplemental material, while two attention plots are shown in Figure 2. Figure 2b demonstrates a common pathology of the model, where a phrasal encoder constituent would be attended to during decoding of the head word of the corresponding decoder constituent, while the head word of the encoder constituent would be attended to during decoding of the decoder constituent corresponding to the whole phrase. Another common pathology is repeated sentence fragments in the translation, which are likely generated because the model cannot condition future attention directly on past attention weights (the "input feeding" approach introduced by Luong et al. (2015)).

Translation quality also suffers because of our use of a stack-only RNNG, which we chose because an RNNG with both stack and buffer inputs is incompatible with a language model loss. During encoding, the model must decide at the very beginning of the sentence how deeply to embed the first character. But with a stack-only RNNG, it must make this decision randomly, since it isn't able to use the buffer representation—which contains the entire sentence.

4 Conclusion

We introduce a new approach to leveraging unsupervised tree structures in NLP tasks like machine translation. Our experiments demonstrate that a small-scale MT dataset contains sufficient training signal to infer latent linguistic structure, and we are excited to learn what models like the one presented here can discover in full-size translation corpora. One particularly promising avenue of research is to leverage the inherently compositional phrase representations $\mathbf{h}_i^{\text{enc}}$ produced by the encoder for other NLP tasks.

There are also many possible directions for improving the model itself and the training process. Value function baselines can replace exponential moving averages, pure reinforcement learning can replace teacher forcing, and beam search can be used in place of greedy inference. Solutions to the translation pathologies presented in Section 3 are likely more complex, although one possible approach would leverage variational inference using a teacher model that can see the buffer and helps train a stack-only student model.

References

Samuel Bowman, Jon Gauthier, Abhinav Rastogi, Raghav Gupta, Christopher Manning, and Christopher Potts. 2016. A fast unified model for parsing and sentence understanding. In *ACL*.

David Chiang. 2005. A hierarchical phrase-based model for statistical machine translation. In *ACL*.

Junyoung Chung, Sungjin Ahn, and Yoshua Bengio. 2017. Hierarchical multiscale recurrent neural networks. In *ICLR*.

Chris Dyer, Miguel Ballesteros, Wang Ling, Austin Matthews, and Noah A Smith. 2016a. Transition-based dependency parsing with stack long short-term memory. In *EMNLP*.

Chris Dyer, Adhiguna Kuncoro, Miguel Ballesteros, and Noah Smith. 2016b. Recurrent neural network grammars. In *NAACL*.

Akiko Eriguchi, Kazuma Hashimoto, and Yoshimasa Tsuruoka. 2016. Tree-to-sequence attentional neural machine translation. In *ACL*.

Akiko Eriguchi, Yoshimasa Tsuruoka, and Kyunghyun Cho. 2017. Learning to parse and translate improves neural machine translation. *arXiv preprint arXiv:1702.03525* .

Christoph Goller and Andreas Küchler. 1996. Learning task-dependent distributed representations by backpropagation through structure. In *IEEE International Conference on Neural Networks*. IEEE, volume 1, pages 347–352.

Kazuma Hashimoto and Yoshimasa Tsuruoka. 2017. Neural machine translation with source-side latent graph parsing. *arXiv preprint arXiv:1702.02265* .

Liang Huang, Kevin Knight, and Aravind Joshi. 2006. A syntax-directed translator with extended domain of locality. In *CHPJI-NLP*. Association for Computational Linguistics.

Yoon Kim, Carl Denton, Luong Hoang, and Alexander Rush. 2017. Structured attention networks. In *ICLR*.

Diederik Kingma and Jimmy Ba. 2015. Adam: A method for stochastic optimization. In *ICLR*.

G. Klein, Y. Kim, Y. Deng, J. Senellart, and A. M. Rush. 2017. OpenNMT: Open-source toolkit for neural machine translation. *ArXiv preprint arXiv:1701.02810* .

Adhiguna Kuncoro, Miguel Ballesteros, Lingpeng Kong, Chris Dyer, Graham Neubig, and Noah Smith. 2017. What do recurrent neural network grammars learn about syntax? In *EACL*.

Minh-Thang Luong, Hieu Pham, and Christopher D Manning. 2015. Effective approaches to attention-based neural machine translation. In *EMNLP*.

Maria Nadejde, Siva Reddy, Rico Sennrich, Tomasz Dwojak, Marcin Junczys-Dowmunt, Philipp Koehn, and Alexandra Birch. 2017. Syntax-aware neural machine translation using ccg. *arXiv preprint arXiv:1702.01147* .

Jordan B Pollack. 1990. Recursive distributed representations. *Artificial Intelligence* 46(1):77–105.

John Schulman, Nicolas Heess, Theophane Weber, and Pieter Abbeel. 2015. Gradient estimation using stochastic computation graphs. In *NIPS*.

Rico Sennrich and Barry Haddow. 2016. Linguistic input features improve neural machine translation. In *WMT*.

Richard Socher, Christopher Manning, and Andrew Ng. 2010. Learning continuous phrase representations and syntactic parsing with recursive neural networks. In *NIPS Workshop on Deep Learning and Unsupervised Feature Learning*.

Richard Socher, Alex Perelygin, Jean Wu, Jason Chuang, Christopher Manning, Andrew Ng, and Christopher Potts. 2013. Recursive deep models for semantic compositionality over a sentiment treebank. In *EMNLP*.

Lucia Specia, Stella Frank, Khalil Simaan, and Desmond Elliott. 2016. A shared task on multimodal machine translation and crosslingual image description. In *WMT*.

Dekai Wu. 1997. Stochastic inversion transduction grammars and bilingual parsing of parallel corpora. *Computational linguistics* 23(3):377–403.

Dani Yogatama, Phil Blunsom, Chris Dyer, Edward Grefenstette, and Wang Ling. 2017. Learning to compose words into sentences with reinforcement learning. In *ICLR*.

Structured Prediction via Learning to Search under Bandit Feedback

Amr Sharaf and **Hal Daumé III**
University of Maryland, College Park
{amr,hal}@cs.umd.edu

Abstract

We present an algorithm for structured prediction under online bandit feedback. The learner repeatedly predicts a sequence of actions, generating a structured output. It then observes feedback for that output and no others. We consider two cases: a pure bandit setting in which it only observes a loss, and more fine-grained feedback in which it observes a loss for every action. We find that the fine-grained feedback is necessary for strong empirical performance, because it allows for a robust variance-reduction strategy. We empirically compare a number of different algorithms and exploration methods and show the efficacy of BLS on sequence labeling and dependency parsing tasks.

1 Introduction

In structured prediction the goal is to jointly predict the values of a collection of variables that interact. In the usual "supervised" setting, at training time, you have access to ground truth outputs (e.g., dependency trees) on which to build a predictor. We consider the substantially harder case of online *bandit* structured prediction, in which the system never sees supervised training data, but instead must make predictions and then only receives feedback about the quality of that *single* prediction. The model we simulate (Figure 1) is:

1. the world reveals an input (e.g., a sentence)
2. the algorithm produces a *single* structured prediction (e.g., full parse tree);
3. the world provides a loss (e.g., overall quality rating) and possibly a small amount of additional feedback;
4. the algorithm updates itself

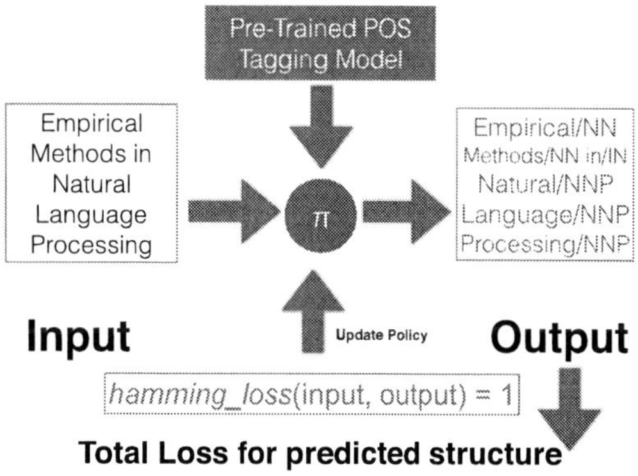

Figure 1: BLS for learning POS tagging. We learn a policy π, whose output a user sees. The user views predicted tags and provides a loss (and possibly additional feedback, such as which words are labeled incorrectly). This is used to update π.

The goal of the system is to minimize it's cumulative loss over time, using the feedback to improve itself. This introduces a fundamental exploration-versus-exploitation trade-off, in which the system must try new things in hopes that it will learn something useful, but also in which it is penalized (by high cumulative loss) for exploring too much.[1]

One natural question we explore in this paper is: in addition to the loss, what forms of feedback are both easy for a user to provide and useful for a system to utilize? At one extreme, one can solicit no additional feedback, which makes the learning problem very difficult. We describe *Bandit Learning to Search*, BLS[2], an approach for improving joint predictors from different types of bandit feedback. The algorithm predicts outputs and observes the loss of the predicted struc-

[1]Unlike active learning—in which the system chooses which examples it wants feedback on—in our setting the system is beholden to the human's choice in inputs.

[2]Our implementation will be made freely available.

Proceedings of the 2nd Workshop on Structured Prediction for Natural Language Processing, pages 17–26
Copenhagen, Denmark, September 7–11, 2017.

ture; but then it uses a regression strategy to estimate *counterfactual* costs of (some) other structures that it did *not* predict. This variance reduction technique (§2.2) is akin to doubly-robust estimation in contextual bandits. The trade-off is that in order to accurately train these regressors, BLS requires per-action feedback from the user (e.g., which words were labeled incorrectly). It appears that this feedback is necessary; with out it, accuracy *degrades* over time. Additionally, we consider several forms of exploration beyond a simple ϵ-greedy strategy, including Boltzmann exploration and Thompson sampling (§2.4). We demonstrate the efficacy of these developments on POS tagging, syntactic chunking and dependency parsing (§ 3), in which we show improvements over both LOLS (Chang et al., 2015) and Policy Gradient (Sutton et al., 1999).

2 Learning with Bandit Feedback

We operate in the learning to search framework, a family of algorithms for solving structured prediction problems, which essentially train a *policy* to make sequence of decisions that are stitched together into a final structured output. Such algorithms decompose a joint prediction task into a sequence of action predictions, such as predicting the label of the next word in sequence labeling or predicting a shift/reduce action in dependency parsing[3]; these predictions are tied by features and/or internal state. Algorithms in this family have recently met with success in neural networks (Bengio et al., 2015; Wiseman and Rush, 2016), though date back to models typically based on linear policies (Collins and Roark, 2004; Daumé III and Marcu, 2005; Xu et al., 2007; Daumé III et al., 2009; Ross et al., 2010; Ross and Bagnell, 2014; Doppa et al., 2014; Chang et al., 2015).

Most learning to search algorithms operate by considering a search space like that shown in Figure 2. The learning algorithm first *rolls-in* for a few steps using a *roll-in* policy π^{in} to some state R, then considers all possible actions available at state R, and then *rolls out* using a *roll-out* policy π^{out} until the end of the sequence. In the fully supervised case, the learning algorithm can then compute a loss for all possible outputs, and use this loss to drive learning at state R, by encouraging the learner to take the action with lowest cost, updating the learned policy from $\hat{\pi}_i$ to $\hat{\pi}_{i+1}$.

[3]Although the decomposition is into a sequence of predictions, such approaches are not limited to "left-to-right" style prediction tasks (Ross et al., 2010; Stoyanov et al., 2011).

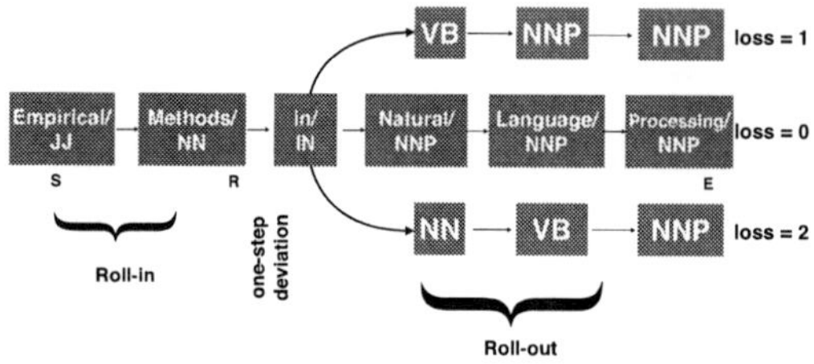

Figure 2: A search space for part of speech tagging, explored by a policy that chooses to "explore" at state R.

In the bandit setting, this is not possible: we can only evaluate one loss; nevertheless, we can follow a similar algorithmic structure. Our specific algorithm, BLS, is summarized in algorithm 1. We start with a pre-trained reference policy π^{ref} and seek to improve it with bandit feedback. On each example, an exploration algorithm (§2.4) chooses whether to explore or exploit. If it chooses to exploit, a random learned policy is used to make a prediction and no updates are made. If, instead, it chooses to explore, it executes a roll-in as usual, a *single* deviation at time t according to the exploration policy, and then a roll-out. Upon completion it suffers a bandit loss for the *entire* complete trajectory. It then uses a *cost estimator* ρ to guess the costs of the un-taken actions. From this it forms a complete cost vector, and updates the underlying policy based on this cost vector. Finally, it updates the cost estimator ρ.

2.1 Cost Estimation by Importance Sampling

The simplest possible method of cost estimation is importance sampling (Horvitz and Thompson, 1952; Chang et al., 2015). If the third action is the one explored with probability p_3 and a cost $\hat{c}_3$ is observed, then the cost vector for all actions is set to $\langle 0, 0, \hat{c}_3/p_3, 0, \ldots, 0 \rangle$. This yields an unbiased estimate of the true cost vector because in expectation over all possible actions, the cost vector equals $\langle \hat{c}_1, \hat{c}_2, \ldots, \hat{c}_K \rangle$.

Unfortunately, this type of cost estimate suffers from huge variance (see experiments in §3). If actions are explored uniformly at random, then all cost vectors look like $\langle 0, 0, K\hat{c}_3, 0, \ldots 0 \rangle$, which varies quite far from its expectation when K is large. To better understand the variance reduction issue, consider the part of speech tagging exam-

Input: examples $\{x_i\}_{i=1}^N$, reference policy π^{ref}, exploration algorithm *explorer*, and rollout-parameter $\beta \geq 0$

$\pi_0 \leftarrow$ initial policy
$\mathcal{I} \leftarrow \emptyset$
$\rho \leftarrow$ initial cost estimator
for *each x_i in training examples* **do**
  if *explorer* chooses not to explore **then**
    $\pi \leftarrow$ *Unif*($\mathcal{I}$) // pick policy
    $y_i \leftarrow$ predict using π
    $c \leftarrow$ bandit loss of y_i
  else
    $t \leftarrow$ *Unif*$(0, T-1)$ // deviation time
    $\tau \leftarrow$ roll-in with $\hat{\pi}_i$ for t rounds
    $s_t \leftarrow$ final state in τ
    $a_t =$ *explorer*(s_t) // deviation action
    $\pi^{\text{out}} \leftarrow \pi^{\text{ref}}$ with prob β, else $\hat{\pi}_i$
    $y_i \leftarrow$ roll-out with π^{out} from $\tau + a_t$
    $c \leftarrow$ bandit loss of y_i
    $\hat{c} \leftarrow$ *est_cost*$(s_t, \tau, \rho, A(s_t), a_t, c)$
    $\hat{\pi}_{i+1} \leftarrow$ *update*$(\hat{\pi}_i, (\Phi(x_i, s_t), \hat{c}))$
    $\mathcal{I} \leftarrow \mathcal{I} \cup \{\hat{\pi}_{i+1}\}$
    update cost estimator ρ
  end
end

Algorithm 1: Bandit Learning to Search (BLS)

Input: current state: s_t; roll-in trajectory: τ; K regression functions (one for every action): ρ; set of allowed actions: $A(s_t)$; roll-out policy: π^{out}; explored action: a_t; bandit loss: c

$t \leftarrow |\tau|$
Initialize $\hat{c}$: a vector of size $|A(s_t)|$
$\hat{c}_0 \leftarrow 0$
for $(a, s) \in \tau$ **do**
  $\hat{c}_0 \leftarrow \hat{c}_0 + \rho_a(\Phi(s))$
end
for $a \in A(s_t)$ **do**
  if $a = a_t$ **then**
    $\hat{c}(a) \leftarrow c$
  else
    $\hat{c}(a) \leftarrow \hat{c}_0$
    $y \leftarrow$ roll-out with π^{out} from $\tau + a$
    for (a', s') *in* y **do**
      $\hat{c}(a) \leftarrow \hat{c}(a) + \rho_{a'}(\Phi(s'))$
    end
end
return $\hat{c}$: *a vector of size* $|A(s_t)|$, *where* $\hat{c}(a)$ *is the estimated cost for action a at state s_t.*

Algorithm 2: *est_cost*

ple from Figure 2. As in the figure, suppose that the deviation occurs at time step 3 and that during roll-in, the first two words are tagged correctly by the roll-in policy. At $t = 3$, there are 45 possible actions (each possible part of speech) to take from the deviation state, of which three are shown; each action (under uniform exploration) will be taken with probability $1/45$. If the first is taken, a loss of one will be observed, if the second, a loss of zero, and if the third, a loss of two. When a fair coin is flipped, perhaps the third choice is selected, which will induce a cost vector of $\vec{c} = \langle 0, 0, 90, 0, \dots \rangle$. In expectation over this random choice, we have $\mathbb{E}_a[c]$ is correct, implying unbiasedness, but the variance is very large: $\mathcal{O}((Kc_{\max})^2)$.

This problem is exacerbated by the fact that many learning to search algorithms define the cost of an action a to be the *difference* between the cost of a and the minimum cost. This is desirable because when the policy is predicting greedily, it should choose the action that *adds* the least cost; it should not need to account for already-incurred cost. For example, suppose the first two words in Figure 2 were tagged incorrectly. This would add a loss of 2 to any of the estimated costs, but could be very difficult to fit because this loss was based on past actions, not the current action.

2.2 Doubly Robust Cost Estimation

To address the challenge of high variance cost estimates, we adopt a strategy similar to the doubly-robust estimation used in the (non-structured) contextual bandit setting (Dudik et al., 2011). In particular, we train a separate set of regressors to estimate the total costs of any action, which we use to impute a counterfactual cost for untaken actions.

Algorithm 2 spells this out, taking advantage of an action-to-cost regressor, ρ. To estimate the cost of an un-taken action a' at a deviation, we simulate the execution of a', followed by the execution of the current policy through the end. The cost of that entire trajectory is estimated by summing ρ over all states along the path. For example, in the part of speech tagging example above, we learn 45 regressors: one for each part of speech. The cost of a roll-out is estimated as the sum of these regressors over the entire predicted sequence.

Using this doubly-robust estimate strategy addresses *both* of the problems mentioned in §2.1.

First, this is able to provide a cost estimate for *all* actions. Second, because ρ is deterministic, it will give the same cost to the common prefix of all trajectories, thus resolving credit assignment.

The remaining challenge is: how to estimate these regressors. Unfortunately, this currently comes at an additional cost to the user: we must observe per-action feedback. In particular, when the user views a predicted output (e.g., part of speech sequence), we ask for a binary signal for each action whether the predicted action was right or wrong. Thus, for a sentence of length T, we generate T training examples for every time step $1 \leq t \leq T$. Each training example has the form: (a_t, c_t), where a_t is the predicted action at time t, and c_t is a binary cost, either 1 if the predicted action was correct, or zero otherwise. This amounts to a user "crossing out" errors, which hopefully incurs low overhead. Using these T training examples, we can effectively train the K regressors for estimating the cost of unobserved actions.

2.3 Theoretical Analysis

In order to analyze the variance of the BLS estimator (in particular to demonstrate that it has lower variance than importance sampling), we provide a reduction to contextual bandits in an i.i.d setting. Dudík et al. (2014) studied the contextual bandit setting, which is similar to out setting but without the complexity of *sequences* of actions. (In particular, if $T = 1$ then our setting is exactly the contextual bandit setting.) They studied the task of off-policy evaluation and optimization for a target policy ν using doubly robust estimation given historic data from an exploration policy μ consisting of contexts, actions, and received rewards. They prove that this approach yields accurate value estimates when there is either a good (but not necessarily consistent) model of rewards or a good (but not necessarily consistent) model of past policy. In particular, they show:

Theorem. *Let $\Delta(x, a)$ and $\rho_k(x, a)$ denote, respectively, the additive error of the reward estimator $\hat{r}$ and the multiplicative error of the action probability estimator $\hat{\mu}_k$. If exploration policy μ and the estimator $\hat{\mu}_k$ are stationary, and the target policy ν is deterministic, then the variance of the doubly robust estimator $\mathbb{V}_\mu[\hat{V}_{DR}]$ is:*

$$\frac{1}{n}(\mathbb{V}_{(x,a)\sim\nu}[r^*(x,a) + (1-\rho_1(x,a))\Delta(x,a)])$$
$$+\mathbb{E}_{(x,a)\sim\nu}[\frac{1}{\hat{\mu}_1(a|x)}\rho_1(x,a)\mathbb{V}_{r\sim D(\cdot|x,a)}[r]]$$
$$+\mathbb{E}_{(x,a)\sim\nu}[\frac{1-\mu_1(a|x)}{\hat{\mu}_1(a|x)}\rho_1(x,a)\Delta(x,a)^2]]$$

The theorem show that the variance can be decomposed into three terms. The first term accounts for the randomness in the context features. The second term accounts for randomness in rewards and disappears when rewards are deterministic functions of the context and actions. The last term accounts for the disagreement between actions taken by the exploration policy μ and the target policy ν. This decomposition shows that doubly robust estimation yields accurate value estimates when there is either a good model of rewards or a good model of the exploration policy.

We can build on this result for BLS to show an *identical* result under the following reduction. The exploration policy μ in our setting is defined as follows: for every exploration round, a randomly selected time-step is assigned a randomly chosen action, and a deterministic reference policy is used to generate the roll-in and roll-out trajectories. Our goal is to evaluate and optimize a better target policy ν. Under this setting, and assuming that the structures are generated i.i.d from a fixed but unknown distribution, the structured prediction problem will be equivalent to a contextual bandit problem were we consider the roll-in trajectory as part of the context.

2.4 Options for Exploration Strategies

In addition to the ϵ-greedy exploration algorithm, we consider the following exploration strategies:

Boltzmann (Softmax) Exploration. Boltzmann exploration varies the action probabilities as a graded function of estimated value. The greedy action is still given the highest selection probability, but all the others are ranked and weighted according to their cost estimates; action a is chosen with probability proportional to $\exp\left[\frac{1}{\text{temp}}c(a)\right]$, where "temp" is a positive parameter called the temperature, and $c(a)$ is the current predicted cost of taking action a. High temperatures cause the actions to be all (nearly) equiprobable. Low temperatures cause a greater difference in selection probability for actions that differ in their value estimates.

Thompson Sampling estimates the following elements: a set Θ of parameters μ; a prior distribution $P(\mu)$ on these parameters; past observations D consisting of observed contexts and rewards; a likelihood function $P(r|b,\mu)$, which gives the probability of reward given a context b and a parameter μ; In each round, Thompson Sampling selects an action according to its posterior probability of having the best parameter μ. This is achieved by taking a sample of parameter for each action, using the posterior distributions, and selecting that action that produces the best sample (Agrawal and Goyal, 2013; Komiyama et al., 2015). We use Gaussian likelihood function and Gaussian prior for the Thompson Sampling algorithm. In addition, we make a linear payoff assumption similar to (Agrawal and Goyal, 2013), where we assume that there is an unknown underlying parameter $\mu_a \in R^d$ such that the expected cost for each action a, given the state s_t and context x_i is $\Phi(x_i, s_t)^T \mu_a$.

3 Experimental Results

The evaluation framework we consider is the fully online setup described in the introduction, measuring the degree to which various algorithms can effectively improve upon a reference policy by observing only a partial feedback signal, and effectively balancing exploration and exploitation. We learn from one structured example at every time step, and we do a single pass over the available examples. We measure loss as the average cumulative loss over time, thus algorithms are appropriately "penalized" for unnecessary exploration.

3.1 Tasks, Policy Classes and Data Sets

We experiment with the following three tasks. For each, we briefly define the problem, describe the policy class that we use for solving that problem in a learning to search framework (we adopt a similar setting to that of (Chang et al., 2016), who describes the policies in more detail), and describe the data sets that we use. The regression problems are solved using squared error regression, and the classification problems (policy learning) is solved via cost-sensitive one-against-all.

Part-Of-Speech Tagging over the 45 Penn Treebank (Marcus et al., 1993) tags. To simulate a domain adaptation setting, we train a reference policy on the TweetNLP dataset (Owoputi et al., 2013), which achieves good accuracy in domain, but does poorly out of domain. We simulate bandit feedback over the entire Penn Treebank Wall Street Journal (sections 02–21 and 23), comprising $42k$ sentences and about one million words. (Adapting *from* tweets *to* WSJ is nonstandard; we do it here because we need a large dataset on which to simulate bandit feedback.) The measure of performance is average per-word accuracy (one minus Hamming loss).

Noun Phrase Chunking is a sequence segmentation task, in which sentences are divided into base noun phrases.We solve this problem using a sequence span identification predictor based on Begin-In-Out encoding, following (Ratinov and Roth, 2009), though applied to chunking rather than named-entity recognition. We used the CoNLL-2000 datasetfor training and testing. We used the smaller test split ($2,012$ sentences) for training a reference policy, and used the training split ($8,500$ sentences) for online evaluation. Performance was measured by F-score over predicted noun phrases (for which one has to predict the entire noun phrase correctly to get any points).

Dependency Parsing is a syntactic analysis task, in which each word in a sentence gets assigned a grammatical head (or "parent"). The experimental setup is similar to part-of-speech tagging. We train an arc-eager dependency parser (Nivre, 2003), which chooses among (at most) four actions at each state: Shift, Reduce, Left or Right. As in part of speech tagging, the reference policy is trained on the TweetNLP dataset (using an oracle due to (Goldberg and Nivre, 2013)), and evaluated on the Penn Treebank corpus (again, sections $02-21$ and section 23). The loss is unlabeled attachment score (UAS), which measures the fraction of words that pick the correct parent.

3.2 Main Results

Here, we describe experimental results (Table 1) comparing several algorithms: (line B) The bandit variant of the LOLS algorithm, which uses importance sampling and ϵ-greedy exploration; (lines C-F) BLS, with bandit feedback and per-word error correction, with variance reduction and four exploration strategies: ϵ-greedy, Boltzmann, Thompson, and "oracle" exploration in which case the oracle action is always chosen during exploration; (line G) The Policy Gradient reinforcement learning algorithm, with ϵ-greedy exploration on one-step deviations; and (line H) A fully super-

Algorithm	Variant	POS Acc	DepPar UAS	Chunk F-Scr
A. Reference	-	47.24	44.15	74.73
B. LOLS	ϵ-greedy	2.29	18.55	31.76
C. BLS	ϵ-greedy	86.55	56.04	90.03
D.	Boltz.	**89.62**	**57.20**	**90.91**
E.	Thomp.	89.37	56.60	90.06
F.	Oracle	89.23	56.60	90.58
G. Policy∇	ϵ-greedy	75.10	-	90.07
H. DAgger	Full Sup	96.51	90.64	95.29

Table 1: Total progressive accuracies for the different algorithms on the three natural language processing tasks. LOLS uniformly *decreases* performance over the Reference baseline. BLS, which integrates cost regressors, uniformly improves, often quite dramatically. The overall effect of the exploration mechanism is small, but in all cases Boltzmann exploration is statistically significantly better than the other options at the $p < 0.05$ level (because the sample size is so large). Policy Gradient for dependency parsing is missing because after processing $\frac{1}{4}$ of the data, it was substantially subpar.

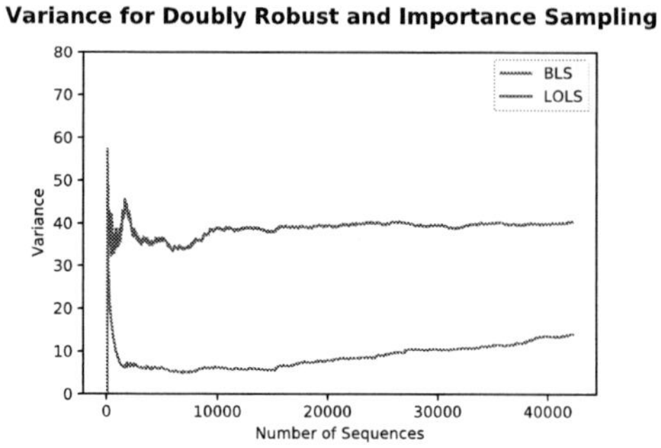

Figure 3: Analyzing the variance of the the cost estimates from LOLS and BLS over a run of the algorithm for POS; the x-axis is number of sentences processed, y-axis is empirical variance.

vised "upper bound" trained with DAgger.

From these results, we draw the following conclusions (the rest of this section elaborates on these conclusions in more detail):

1. The original LOLS algorithm is ineffective at improving the accuracy of a poor reference policy (A vs B);
2. Collecting additional per-word feedback in BLS allows the algorithm to drastically improve on the reference (A vs C) and on LOLS (B vs C); we show in §3.3 that this happens because of variance reduction;
3. Additional leverage can be gained by varying the exploration strategy, and in general Boltzmann exploration is effective (C,D,E), but the Oracle exploration strategy is *not* optimal (F vs D); see §3.4;
4. For large action spaces like POS tagging, the BLS-type updates outperform Policy Gradient-type updates, when the exploration strategy is held constant (G vs D), see §3.5.
5. Bandit feedback is less effective than full feedback (H vs D) (§3.6).

3.3 Effect of Variance Reduction

Table 1 shows the progressive validation accuracies for all three tasks for a variety of algorithmic settings. To understand the effect of variance, it is enough to compare the performance of the Reference policy (the policy learned from the out of domain data) with that of LOLS. In all of these cases, running LOLS substantially decreases performance. Accuracy drops by 45% for POS tagging, 26% for dependency parsing and 43% for noun phrase chunking. For POS tagging, the LOLS accuracy falls *below* the accuracy one would get for random guessing (which is approximately 14% on this dataset for NN)!

When the underlying algorithm changes from LOLS to BLS, the overall accuracies go up significantly. Part of speech tagging accuracy increases from 47% to 86%; dependency parsing accuracy from 44% to 57%; and chunking F-score from 74% to 90%. These numbers naturally fall below state of the art for *fully supervised* learning on these data sets, precisely because these results are based only on bandit feedback (see §3.6).

3.4 Effect of Exploration Strategy

Figure 4 shows the effect of the choice of ϵ for ϵ-greedy exploration in BLS. Overall, best results are achieved with *remarkably* high epsilon, which is possibly counter-intuitive. The reason this happens is because BLS only explores on one out of T time steps, of which there are approximately 30 in each of these experiments (the sentence lengths). This means that even with $\epsilon = 1$, we only take a random action roughly 3.3% of the time. It is therefore not surprising that large ϵ is the most effective strategy. Overall, although the differences are small, the best choice of ϵ across these different tasks is ≈ 0.6.

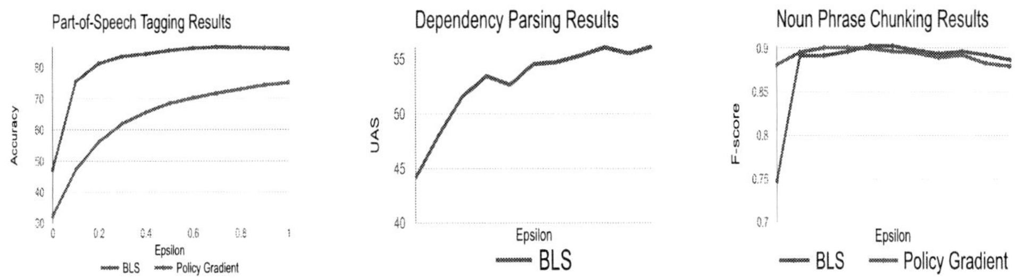

Figure 4: Analyzing the effect of ϵ in exploration/exploitation trade-off. Overall, large values of ϵ are strongly preferred.

Returning to Table 1, we can consider the effect of different exploration mechanisms: ϵ-greedy, Boltzmann (or softmax) exploration, and Thompson sampling. Overall, Boltzmann exploration was the most effective strategy, gaining about 3% accuracy in POS tagging, just over 1% in dependency parsing, and just shy of 1% in noun phrase chunking. Although the latter two effects are small, they are statistically significant, which is measurable due to the fact that the evaluation sets are very large. In general, Thompson sampling is also effective, though worse than Boltzmann.

Finally, we consider a variant in which whenever BLS requests exploration, the algorithm "cheats" and chooses the gold standard decision at that point. This is the "oracle exploration" line in Table 1. We see that this does *not* improve overall quality, which suggests that a good exploration strategy is not one that always does the right thing, but one that also explored bad—but useful-to-learn-from—options.

3.5 Policy Gradient Updates

A natural question is: how does bandit structured prediction compare to more standard approaches to reinforcement learning (we revisit the question of how these problems differ in § 4). We chose Policy Gradient (Sutton et al., 1999) as a point of comparison. The main question we seek to address is how the BLS update rule compares to the Policy Gradient update rule. In order to perform this comparison, we hold the exploration strategy *fixed*, and implement the Policy Gradient update rule inside our system.

More formally, the policy gradient optimization is similar to that used in BLS. PG maintains a policy π_θ, which is parameterized by a set of parameters θ. Features are extracted from each state s_t to construct the feature vectors $\phi(s_t)$, and linear function approximation models the probability of selecting action a_t at state s_t under π_θ: $\pi_\theta(a_t|s_t) \propto \exp(\theta_{a_t}^T \phi(s_t))$, where K is the total number of actions. PG maximizes the total expected return under the distribution of trajectories sampled from the policy π_θ.

To balance the exploration / exploitation trade-off, we use exactly the same epsilon greedy technique used in BLS (Algorithm 1). For each trajectory τ sampled from π_θ, a state is selected uniformly at random, and an action is selected greedily with probability ϵ. The policy π_θ is used to construct the roll-in and roll-out trajectories. For every trajectory τ, we collect the same binary grades from the user as in BLS, and use them to train a regression function to estimate the per-step reward. These estimates are then be summed up to compute the total return G_t from time step t onwards (Algorithm 2).

We use standard policy gradient update for optimizing the policy θ based on the observed rewards:

$$\theta \leftarrow \theta + \alpha \nabla_\theta \log(\pi_\theta(s_t, a_t)) G_t \qquad (1)$$

The results of this experiment are shown in line G of Table 1. Here, we see that on POS tagging, where the number of actions is very large, PG significantly underperforms BLS. Our initial experiments in dependency parsing showed the PG significantly underperformed BLS after processing $\frac{1}{4}$ of the data. The difference is substantially smaller in chunking, where PG is on part with BLS with ϵ-greedy exploration. Figure 4 shows the effect of ϵ on PG, where we see that it also prefers large values of ϵ, but its performance saturates as $\epsilon \rightarrow 1$.

3.6 Bandit Feedback vs Full Feedback

Finally, we consider the trade-off between bandit feedback in BLS and full feedback. To make this comparison, we run the fully supervised algorithm DAgger (Ross et al., 2010) which is effectively the same algorithm as LOLS and BLS under full supervision. In Table 1, we can see that full supervision dramatically improves performance from around 90% to 97% in POS tagging, 57% to 91% in dependency parsing, and 91% to 95% in chunking. Of course, achieving this improved performance comes at a high labeling cost: a human has to provide exact labels for each decision, not just binary "yes/no" labels.

4 Discussion & Conclusion

The most similar algorithm to ours is the bandit version of LOLS (Chang et al., 2015) (which is analyzed theoretically but not empirically); the key differences between BLS and LOLS are: (a) BLS employs a doubly-robust estimator for "guessing" the costs of counterfactual actions; (b) BLS employs alternative exploration strategies; (c) BLS is effective in practice at improving the performance of an initial policy.

In the NLP community, Sokolov et al. (2016a) and Sokolov et al. (2016b) have proposed a policy gradient-like method for optimizing log-linear models like conditional random fields (Lafferty et al., 2001) under bandit feedback. Their evaluation is most impressive on the problem of domain adaptation of a machine translation system, in which they show that their approach is able to learn solely from bandit-style feedback, though requiring a large number of samples.

In the learning-to-search setting, the difference between *structured prediction under bandit feedback* and *reinforcement learning* gets blurry. A distinction in the problem definition is that the world is typically assumed to be fixed and stochastic in RL, while the world is both deterministic and *known* (conditioned on the input, which is random) in bandit structured prediction: given a state and action, the algorithm always knows what the next state will be. A difference in solution is that there has been relatively little work in reinforcement learning that explicitly begins with a reference policy to improve and often assumes an *ab initio* training regime. In practice, in large state spaces, this makes the problem almost impossible, and practical settings like AlphaGo (Silver et al., 2016) require imitation learning to initialize a good policy, after which reinforcement learning is used to improve that policy.

Learning from partial feedback has generated a vast amount of work in the literature, dating back to the seminal introduction of multi-armed bandits by (Robbins, 1985). However, the vast number of papers on this topic does not consider joint prediction tasks; see (Auer et al., 2002; Auer, 2003; Langford and Zhang, 2008; Srinivas et al., 2009; Li et al., 2010; Beygelzimer et al., 2010; Dudik et al., 2011; Chapelle and Li, 2011; Valko et al., 2013) and references *inter alia*. There, the system observes (bandit) feedback for every decision.

Other forms of contextual bandits on structured problems have been considered recently. Kalai and Vempala (2005) studied the structured problem of online shortest paths, where one has a directed graph and a fixed pair of nodes (s, t). Each period, one has to pick a path from s to t, and then the times on all the edges are revealed. The goal of the learner is to improve it's path predictions over time. Relatedly, Krishnamurthy et al. (2015) studied a variant of the contextual bandit problem, where on each round, the learner plays a sequence of actions, receives a score for each individual action, and obtains a final reward that is a linear combination to those scores.

In this paper, we presented a computationally efficient algorithm for structured contextual bandits, BLS, by combining: locally optimal learning to search (to control the structure of exploration) and doubly robust cost estimation (to control the variance of the cost estimation). This provides the first practically applicable learning to search algorithm for learning from bandit feedback. Unfortunately, this comes at a cost to the user: they must make more fine-grained judgments of correctness than in a full bandit setting. In particular, they must mark each decision as correct or incorrect:it is an open question whether this feedback can be removed without incurring a substantially larger sample complexity. A second large open question is whether the time step at which to deviate can be chosen more intelligently, similar to selective sampling (Shi et al., 2015), using active learning.

Acknowledgements

We thank the anonymous reviewers for many helpful comments. This work was supported by NSF grant IIS-1618193 and LTS grant DO-0032. Opinions, findings, conclusions, or recommendations expressed here are those of the authors and do not necessarily reflect the view of the sponsor(s).

References

Shipra Agrawal and Navin Goyal. 2013. Thompson sampling for contextual bandits with linear payoffs. In *ICML (3)*. pages 127–135.

Peter Auer. 2003. Using confidence bounds for exploitation-exploration trade-offs. *The Journal of Machine Learning Research* 3:397–422.

Peter Auer, Nicolo Cesa-Bianchi, Yoav Freund, and Robert E Schapire. 2002. The nonstochastic multi-armed bandit problem. *SIAM Journal on Computing* 32(1):48–77.

Samy Bengio, Oriol Vinyals, Navdeep Jaitly, and Noam Shazeer. 2015. Scheduled sampling for sequence prediction with recurrent neural networks. In *Advances in Neural Information Processing Systems*. pages 1171–1179.

Alina Beygelzimer, John Langford, Lihong Li, Lev Reyzin, and Robert E Schapire. 2010. Contextual bandit algorithms with supervised learning guarantees. *arXiv preprint arXiv:1002.4058* .

Kai-Wei Chang, He He, Hal Daumé III, John Langford, and Stéphane Ross. 2016. A credit assignment compiler for joint prediction. In *NIPS*.

Kai-Wei Chang, Akshay Krishnamurthy, Alekh Agarwal, Hal Daumé III, and John Langford. 2015. Learning to search better than your teacher. In *Proceedings of The 32nd International Conference on Machine Learning*. pages 2058–2066.

Olivier Chapelle and Lihong Li. 2011. An empirical evaluation of thompson sampling. In *Advances in neural information processing systems*. pages 2249–2257.

Michael Collins and Brian Roark. 2004. Incremental parsing with the perceptron algorithm. In *Proceedings of the 42nd Annual Meeting on Association for Computational Linguistics*. Association for Computational Linguistics, page 111.

Hal Daumé III, John Langford, and Daniel Marcu. 2009. Search-based structured prediction. *Machine learning* 75(3):297–325.

Hal Daumé III and Daniel Marcu. 2005. Learning as search optimization: Approximate large margin methods for structured prediction. In *Proceedings of the 22nd international conference on Machine learning*. ACM, pages 169–176.

Janardhan Rao Doppa, Alan Fern, and Prasad Tadepalli. 2014. Hc-search: A learning framework for search-based structured prediction. *J. Artif. Intell. Res.(JAIR)* 50:369–407.

Miroslav Dudík, Dumitru Erhan, John Langford, Lihong Li, et al. 2014. Doubly robust policy evaluation and optimization. *Statistical Science* 29(4):485–511.

Miroslav Dudik, Daniel Hsu, Satyen Kale, Nikos Karampatziakis, John Langford, Lev Reyzin, and Tong Zhang. 2011. Efficient optimal learning for contextual bandits. *arXiv preprint arXiv:1106.2369* .

Yoav Goldberg and Joakim Nivre. 2013. Training deterministic parsers with non-deterministic oracles. *Transactions of the ACL* 1.

Daniel G Horvitz and Donovan J Thompson. 1952. A generalization of sampling without replacement from a finite universe. *Journal of the American statistical Association* 47(260):663–685.

Adam Kalai and Santosh Vempala. 2005. Efficient algorithms for online decision problems. *Journal of Computer and System Sciences* 71(3):291–307.

Junpei Komiyama, Junya Honda, and Hiroshi Nakagawa. 2015. Optimal regret analysis of thompson sampling in stochastic multi-armed bandit problem with multiple plays. *arXiv preprint arXiv:1506.00779* .

Akshay Krishnamurthy, Alekh Agarwal, and Miroslav Dudik. 2015. Efficient contextual semi-bandit learning. *arXiv preprint arXiv:1502.05890* .

John Lafferty, Andrew McCallum, and Fernando CN Pereira. 2001. Conditional random fields: Probabilistic models for segmenting and labeling sequence data .

John Langford and Tong Zhang. 2008. The epoch-greedy algorithm for multi-armed bandits with side information. In *Advances in neural information processing systems*. pages 817–824.

Lihong Li, Wei Chu, John Langford, and Robert E Schapire. 2010. A contextual-bandit approach to personalized news article recommendation. In *Proceedings of the 19th international conference on World wide web*. ACM, pages 661–670.

Mitchell P Marcus, Mary Ann Marcinkiewicz, and Beatrice Santorini. 1993. Building a large annotated corpus of english: The penn treebank. *Computational linguistics* 19(2):313–330.

Joakim Nivre. 2003. An efficient algorithm for projective dependency parsing. In *IWPT*. pages 149–160.

Olutobi Owoputi, Brendan O'Connor, Chris Dyer, Kevin Gimpel, Nathan Schneider, and Noah A Smith. 2013. Improved part-of-speech tagging for online conversational text with word clusters. Association for Computational Linguistics.

Lev Ratinov and Dan Roth. 2009. Design challenges and misconceptions in named entity recognition. In *CoNLL*.

Herbert Robbins. 1985. Some aspects of the sequential design of experiments. In *Herbert Robbins Selected Papers*, Springer, pages 169–177.

Stephane Ross and J Andrew Bagnell. 2014. Reinforcement and imitation learning via interactive no-regret learning. *arXiv preprint arXiv:1406.5979* .

Stéphane Ross, Geoffrey J Gordon, and J Andrew Bagnell. 2010. A reduction of imitation learning and structured prediction to no-regret online learning. *arXiv preprint arXiv:1011.0686* .

Tianlin Shi, Jacob Steinhardt, and Percy Liang. 2015. Learning where to sample in structured prediction. In *AISTATS*.

David Silver, Aja Huang, Chris J Maddison, Arthur Guez, Laurent Sifre, George Van Den Driessche, Julian Schrittwieser, Ioannis Antonoglou, Veda Panneershelvam, Marc Lanctot, et al. 2016. Mastering the game of go with deep neural networks and tree search. *Nature* 529(7587):484–489.

Artem Sokolov, Julia Kreutzer, Christopher Lo, and Stefan Riezler. 2016a. Learning structured predictors from bandit feedback for interactive NLP. In *Proceedings of the 54th Annual Meeting of the Association for Computational Linguistics (Volume 1: Long Papers)*. Association for Computational Linguistics (ACL). https://doi.org/10.18653/v1/p16-1152.

Artem Sokolov, Stefan Riezler, and Tanguy Urvoy. 2016b. Bandit structured prediction for learning from partial feedback in statistical machine translation. *arXiv preprint arXiv:1601.04468* .

Niranjan Srinivas, Andreas Krause, Sham M Kakade, and Matthias Seeger. 2009. Gaussian process optimization in the bandit setting: No regret and experimental design. *arXiv preprint arXiv:0912.3995* .

Veselin Stoyanov, Alexander Ropson, and Jason Eisner. 2011. Empirical risk minimization of graphical model parameters given approximate inference, decoding, and model structure. In *AISTATS*. pages 725–733.

Richard S Sutton, David A McAllester, Satinder P Singh, Yishay Mansour, et al. 1999. Policy gradient methods for reinforcement learning with function approximation. In *NIPS*. volume 99, pages 1057–1063.

Michal Valko, Nathaniel Korda, Rémi Munos, Ilias Flaounas, and Nelo Cristianini. 2013. Finite-time analysis of kernelised contextual bandits. *arXiv preprint arXiv:1309.6869* .

Sam Wiseman and Alexander M Rush. 2016. Sequence-to-sequence learning as beam-search optimization. *arXiv preprint arXiv:1606.02960* .

Yuehua Xu, Alan Fern, and Sung Wook Yoon. 2007. Discriminative learning of beam-search heuristics for planning. In *IJCAI*. pages 2041–2046.

Syntax Aware LSTM model for Semantic Role Labeling

Feng Qian[2], Lei Sha[1], Baobao Chang[1], Lu-chen Liu[2], Ming Zhang[2*]
[1] Key Laboratory of Computational Linguistics, Ministry of Education
School of Electronics Engineering and Computer Science, Peking University
[2] Institute of Network Computing and Information Systems
School of Electronics Engineering and Computer Science, Peking University
{nickqian, shalei, chbb, liuluchen, mzhang_cs}@pku.edu.cn

Abstract

In Semantic Role Labeling (SRL) task, the tree structured dependency relation is rich in syntax information, but it is not well handled by existing models. In this paper, we propose Syntax Aware Long Short Time Memory (SA-LSTM). The structure of SA-LSTM changes according to dependency structure of each sentence, so that SA-LSTM can model the whole tree structure of dependency relation in an architecture engineering way. Experiments demonstrate that on Chinese Proposition Bank (CPB) 1.0, SA-LSTM improves F_1 by 2.06% than ordinary bi-LSTM with feature engineered dependency relation information, and gives state-of-the-art F_1 of 79.92%. On English CoNLL 2005 dataset, SA-LSTM brings improvement (2.1%) to bi-LSTM model and also brings slight improvement (0.3%) when added to the state-of-the-art model.

1 Introduction

The task of Semantic Role Labeling (SRL) is to recognize arguments of a given predicate in a sentence and assign semantic role labels. Many NLP works such as machine translation (Xiong et al., 2012; Aziz et al., 2011) benefit from SRL because of the semantic structure it provides. Figure 1 shows a sentence with semantic role label.

Dependency relation is considered important for SRL task (Xue, 2008; Punyakanok et al., 2008; Pradhan et al., 2005), since it can provide rich structure and syntax information for SRL. At the bottom of Figure 1 shows dependency of the sentence.

* Corresponding Author

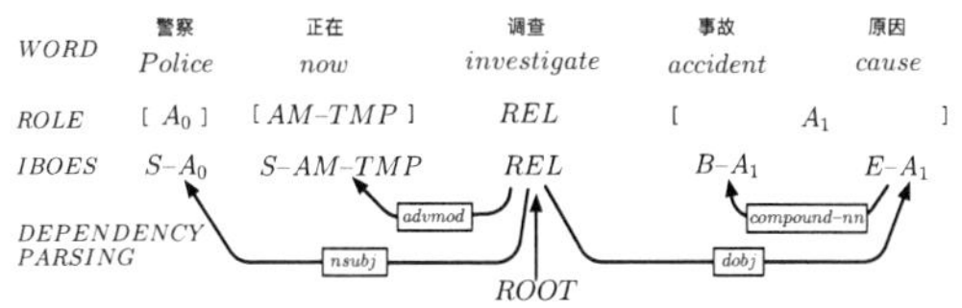

Figure 1: A sentence from Chinese Proposition Bank 1.0 (CPB 1.0) (Xue and Palmer, 2003) with semantic role labels and dependency.

Traditional methods (Sun and Jurafsky, 2004; Xue, 2008; Ding and Chang, 2008, 2009; Sun, 2010) do classification according to manually designed features. Feature engineering requires expertise and is labor intensive. Recent works based on Recurrent Neural Network (RNN) (Zhou and Xu, 2015; Wang et al., 2015; He et al., 2017) extract features automatically, and significantly outperform traditional methods. However, because RNN methods treat language as sequential data, they fail to integrate the tree structured dependency into RNN.

We propose Syntax Aware Long Short Time Memory (SA-LSTM) to directly model complex tree structure of dependency relation in an architecture engineering way. Architecture of SA-LSTM is shown in Figure 2. SA-LSTM is based on bidirectional LSTM (bi-LSTM). In order to model the whole dependency tree, we add additional directed connections between dependency related words in bi-LSTM. SA-LSTM integrates the whole dependency tree directly into the model in an architecture engineering way. Also, to take dependency relation type into account, we introduce trainable weights for different types of dependency relation. The weights can be trained to indicate importance of a dependency type.

SA-LSTM is able to directly model the whole tree structure of dependency relation in an architecture engineering way. Experiments show that

Proceedings of the 2nd Workshop on Structured Prediction for Natural Language Processing, pages 27–32
Copenhagen, Denmark, September 7–11, 2017.

SA-LSTM can model dependency relation better than traditional feature engineering way. SA-LSTM gives state of the art F_1 on CPB 1.0 and also shows improvement on English CoNLL 2005 dataset.

2 Syntax Aware LSTM

In this section, we first introduce ordinary bi-LSTM. Based on bi-LSTM, we then introduce the proposed SA-LSTM. Finally, we introduce how to do optimization for SA-LSTM.

2.1 Conventional bi-LSTM Model for SRL

In a corpus sentence, each word w_t has a feature representation x_t which is generated automatically as (Wang et al., 2015) did. z_t is feature embedding for w_t, calculated as followed:

$$z_t = f(W_1 x_t) \tag{1}$$

where $W_1 \in \mathbb{R}^{n_1 \times n_0}$. n_0 is the dimension of word feature representation.

In a corpus sentence, each word w_t has six internal vectors, $\widetilde{C}$, g_i, g_f, g_o, C_t, and h_t, shown in Equation 2:

$$\begin{aligned} \widetilde{C} &= f(W_c z_t + U_c h_{t-1} + b_c) \\ g_j &= \sigma(W_j z_t + U_j h_{t-1} + b_j) \;\; j \in \{i, f, o\} \\ C_t &= g_i \odot \widetilde{C} + g_f \odot C_{t-1} \\ h_t &= g_o \odot f(C_t) \end{aligned} \tag{2}$$

where $\widetilde{C}$ is the candidate value of the current cell state. g are gates used to control the flow of information. C_t is the current cell state. h_t is hidden state of w_t. W_x and U_x are matrixes used in linear transformation:

$$\begin{aligned} W_x, x \in \{c, i, f, o\} \in \mathbb{R}^{n_h \times n_1} \\ U_x, x \in \{c, i, f, o\} \in \mathbb{R}^{n_h \times n_h} \end{aligned} \tag{3}$$

As convention, f stands for tanh and σ stands for *sigmoid*. $\odot$ means the element-wise multiplication.

In order to make use of bidirectional information, the forward $\overrightarrow{h_t}^T$ and backward $\overleftarrow{h_t}^T$ are concatenated together, as shown in Equation 4:

$$a_t = [\overrightarrow{h_t}^T, \overleftarrow{h_t}^T] \tag{4}$$

Finally, o_t is the result vector with each dimension corresponding to the score of each semantic role tag, and are calculated as shown in Equation 5:

$$o_t = W_3 f(W_2 a_t) \tag{5}$$

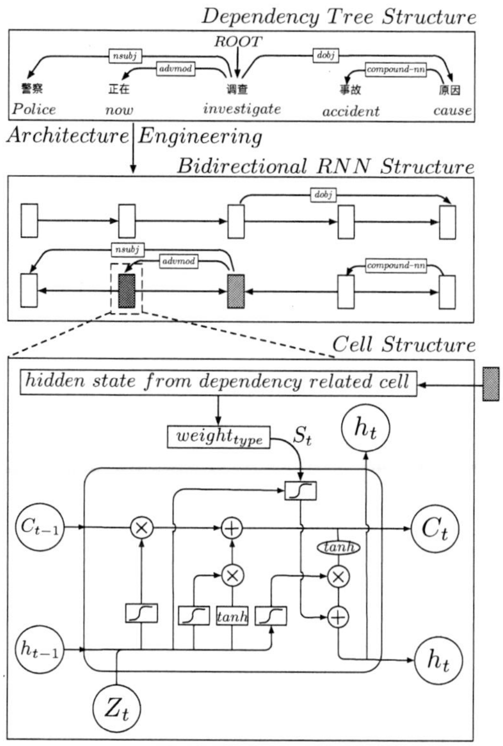

Figure 2: Structure of Syntax Aware LSTM. The purple square is the current cell that is calculating. The green square is a dependency related cell.

where $W_2 \in \mathbb{R}^{n_3 \times n_2}$, n_2 is $2 \times h_t$, $W_3 \in \mathbb{R}^{n_4 \times n_3}$ and n_4 is the number of tags in IOBES tagging schema.

2.2 Syntax Aware LSTM Model for SRL

This section introduces the proposed SA-LSTM model. Figure 2 shows the structure of SA-LSTM. SA-LSTM is based on bidirectional LSTM. By architecture engineering, SA-LSTM can model the whole tree structure of dependency relation.

S_t is the key component of SA-LSTM. It stands for information from other dependency related words, and is calculated as shown in Equation 6:

$$S_t = f(\sum_{i=0}^{t-1} \alpha \times h_i) \tag{6}$$

$$\alpha = \begin{cases} 1 & \text{If there exists dependency} \\ & \text{relation from } w_i \text{ to } w_t \\ 0 & \text{Otherwise} \end{cases} \tag{7}$$

S_t is the weighted sum of all hidden state vectors h_i which come from previous words w_i . Note that, $\alpha \in \{0, 1\}$ indicates whether there is a dependency relation pointed from w_i to w_t.

We add a gate g_s to constrain information from S_t, as shown in Equation 8:

$$g_s = \sigma(W_s z_t + U_s h_{t-1} + b_s) \quad (8)$$

To protect the original word information from being diluted (Wu et al., 2016) by S_t, we add S_t to hidden layer vector h_t instead of adding to cell state C_t. So h_t in SA-LSTM cell is calculated as:

$$h_t = g_o \odot f(C_t) + g_s \odot S_t \quad (9)$$

For example, in Figure 2, there is a dependency relation "advmod" from green square to purple square. By Equation 7, only the hidden state of green square is selected, then transformed by g_s in Equation 8, finally added to hidden layer of the purple cell.

SA-LSTM changes structure by adding different connections according to dependency relation. In this way, SA-LSTM integrates the whole tree structure of dependency.

However, by using α in Equation 7, we do not take dependency type into account, so we further improve the way α is calculated from Equation 7 to Equation 10. Each $type_m$ of dependency relation is assigned a trainable weight α_m. In this way, SA-LSTM can model differences between types of dependency relation.

$$\alpha = \begin{cases} \alpha_m & \text{exists } type_m \text{ dependency} \\ & \text{relation from } w_i \text{ to } w_t \\ 0 & \text{Otherwise} \end{cases} \quad (10)$$

2.3 Optimization

This section introduces optimization methods for SA-LSTM. We use maximum likelihood criterion to train SA-LSTM. We choose stochastic gradient descent algorithm to optimize parameters.

Given a training pair $T = (x, y)$ where T is the current training pair, x denotes current training sentence, and y is the corresponding correct answer path. $y_t = k$ means that the t-th word has the k-th semantic role label.

The score of o_t is calculated as:

$$s(x, y, \theta) = \sum_{t=1}^{N_i} o_{ty_t} \quad (11)$$

where N_i is the word number of the current sentence and θ stands for all parameters. So the log likelihood of a single sentence is:

$$\log p(y|x, \theta) = \log \frac{exp(s(x, y, \theta))}{\sum_{y'} exp(s(x, y', \theta))} \\ = s(x, y, \theta) - log \sum_{y'} exp(s(x, y', \theta)) \quad (12)$$

where y' ranges from all valid paths of answers. We use Viterbi algorithm to calculate the global normalization. Besides, we collected those impossible transitions from corpus beforehand. When calculating global normalization, we prevent calculating impossible paths which contains impossible transitions.

Method	F_1%
Xue(2008)	71.90
Sun et al.(2009)	74.12
Yand and Zong(2014)	75.31
Wang et al.(Bi-LSTM)(2015)	77.09
Sha et al.(2016)	77.69
Path LSTM, Roth et al. (2016)[3]	**79.01**
BiLSTM+feature engineering dependency	77.75
SA-LSTM(**Random Initialized**)	**79.81**
SA-LSTM(**Pre-trained Embedding**)	**79.92**

Table 1: Results comparison on CPB 1.0

3 Experiment

3.1 Experiment setting

In order to compare with previous Chinese SRL works, we choose to do experiment on CPB 1.0. We also follow the same data setting as previous Chinese SRL work (Xue, 2008; Sun et al., 2009) did. Pre-trained[1] word embeddings are tested on SA-LSTM and shows improvement.

For English SRL, we test on CoNLL 2005 dataset.

We use Stanford Parser (Chen and Manning, 2014) to get dependency relation. The training set of Chinese parser overlaps a part of CPB 1.0 test set, so we retrained the parser. Dimension of hyper parameters are tuned according to development set. $n_1 = 200$, $n_h = 100$, $n_2 = 200$, $n_3 = 100$, $learning\ rate = 0.001$.

3.2 Syntax Aware LSTM Performance

To prove that SA-LSTM models dependency relation better than simple feature engineering

[1]Trained by word2vec on Chinese Gigaword Corpus

[2]All experiment code and related files are available on request

[3]We test the model on CPB 1.0

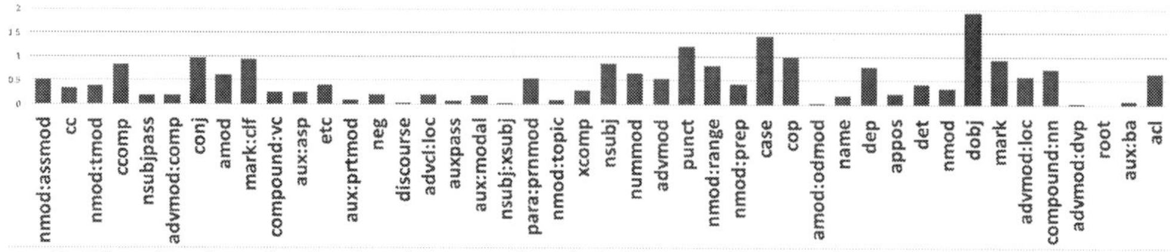

Figure 3: Visualization of trained weight α_m. X axis is Universal Dependency type, Y axis is the weight.

Method	$F_1\%$
Bi-LSTM(2 layers)	74.52
Bi-LSTM + SA-LSTM(2 layers)	**76.63**
He(2017)(Single Model, state of the art)	81.62
He(Single Model, 8 layers) + SA-LSTM	**81.90**

Table 2: Results on English CoNLL 2005

method, we design an experiment in which dependency relation is added to bi-LSTM in a traditional feature engineering way.

Given a word w_t, F_t is the average of all dependency related x_i of previous words w_i, as shown in Equation 13:

$$F_t = \frac{1}{T} \sum_{i=0}^{t-1} \alpha \times x_i \tag{13}$$

where T is the number of dependency related words and α is a $0, 1$ variable calculated as in Equation 7.

Then F_t is concatenated to x_t to form a new feature representation. Then these representations are fed into bi-LSTM.

As shown in Table 1, on CPB 1.0, SA-LSTM reaches $79.81\% F_1$ score with random initialization and $79.92\% F_1$ score with pre-trained word embedding. Both of them are the best F_1 score ever published on CPB 1.0 dataset.

In contrast to the "bi-LSTM+feature engineering dependency" model, it is clear that architecture method of SA-LSTM gains more improvement(77.09% to 79.81%) than simple feature engineering method(77.09% to 77.75%). Path-LSTM (Roth and Lapata, 2016) embeds dependency path between predicate and argument for each word using LSTM, then does classification according to such path embedding and some other features. SA-LSTM ($79.81\% F_1$) outperforms Path-LSTM ($79.01\% F_1$) on CPB 1.0.

Both "bi-LSTM + feature engineering dependency" and Path-LSTM only model dependency parsing information for each single word, which can not model the whole dependency tree structure. However, by building the dependency relation directly into the structure of SA-LSTM and changing the way information flows, SA-LSTM is able to model the whole tree structure of dependency relation.

We also test our SA-LSTM on English CoNLL 2005 dataset. Replacing conventional bi-LSTM by SA-LSTM brings $1.7\% F_1$ improvement. Replacing bi-LSTM layers of the state of the art model (He et al., 2017) by SA-LSTM [1] brings $0.3\% F_1$ improvement.

3.3 Visualization of Trained Weights

According to Equation 10, influence from a single type of dependency relation will be multiplied with type weight α_m. When α_m is 0, the influence from this type of dependency relation will be ignored totally. When the weight is bigger, the type of dependency relation will have more influence on the whole system.

As shown in Figure 3, dependency relation type *dobj* receives the highest weight after training, as shown by the red bar. According to grammar knowledge, *dobj* should be an informative relation for SRL task, and SA-LSTM gives *dobj* the most influence automatically. This further demonstrate that the result of SA-LSTM is highly in accordance with grammar knowledge.

4 Related works

Semantic role labeling (SRL) was first defined by (Gildea and Jurafsky, 2002). Early works (Gildea and Jurafsky, 2002; Sun and Jurafsky, 2004) on SRL got promising result without large annotated SRL corpus. Xue and Palmer (2003) built the Chinese Proposition Bank to standardize Chinese SRL research.

Traditional works such as (Xue and Palmer, 2005; Xue, 2008; Ding and Chang, 2009; Sun et al., 2009; Chen et al., 2006; Yang et al., 2014)

[1] We add syntax-aware connections to every bi-LSTM layer in the 8-layer model of (He et al., 2017)

use feature engineering methods. Their methods can take dependency relation into account in feature engineering way, such as syntactic path feature. It is obvious that feature engineering method can not fully capture the tree structure of dependency relation.

More recent SRL works often use neural network based methods. Collobert and Weston (2008) proposed a Convolutional Neural Network (CNN) method for SRL. Zhou and Xu (2015) proposed bidirectional RNN-LSTM method for English SRL, and Wang et al. (2015) proposed a bi-RNN-LSTM method for Chinese SRL on which SA-LSTM is based. He et al. (2017) further extends the work of Zhou and Xu (2015). NN based methods extract features automatically and significantly outperforms traditional methods. However, most NN based methods can not utilize dependency relation which is considered important for semantic related NLP tasks (Xue, 2008; Punyakanok et al., 2008; Pradhan et al., 2005).

The work of Roth and Lapata (2016) and Sha et al. (2016) have the same motivation as SA-LSTM, but in different ways. Sha et al. (2016) uses dependency relation as feature to do argument relations classification. Roth and Lapata (2016) embeds dependency path into feature representation for each word using LSTM. In contrast, SA-LSTM utilizes dependency relation in an architecture engineering way, by integrating the whole dependency tree structure directly into SA-LSTM structure.

5 Conclusion

We propose Syntax Aware LSTM model for Semantic Role Labeling (SRL). SA-LSTM is able to directly model the whole tree structure of dependency relation in an architecture engineering way. Experiments show that SA-LSTM can model dependency relation better than traditional feature engineering way. SA-LSTM gives state of the art F_1 on CPB 1.0 and also shows improvement on English CoNLL 2005 dataset.

Acknowledgments

Thanks Natali for proofreading the paper and giving so many valuable suggestions.

This paper is partially supported by the National Natural Science Foundation of China (NSFC Grant Nos. 61472006 and 91646202) as well as the National Basic Research Program (973 Program No. 2014CB340405).

References

Wilker Aziz, Miguel Rios, and Lucia Specia. 2011. Shallow semantic trees for smt. In *Proceedings of the Sixth Workshop on Statistical Machine Translation*, pages 316–322. Association for Computational Linguistics.

Danqi Chen and Christopher D Manning. 2014. A fast and accurate dependency parser using neural networks. In *EMNLP*, pages 740–750.

Wenliang Chen, Yujie Zhang, and Hitoshi Isahara. 2006. An empirical study of chinese chunking. In *Proceedings of the COLING/ACL on Main conference poster sessions*, pages 97–104. Association for Computational Linguistics.

Ronan Collobert and Jason Weston. 2008. A unified architecture for natural language processing: Deep neural networks with multitask learning. In *Proceedings of the 25th international conference on Machine learning*, pages 160–167. ACM.

Weiwei Ding and Baobao Chang. 2008. Improving chinese semantic role classification with hierarchical feature selection strategy. In *Proceedings of the conference on empirical methods in natural language processing*, pages 324–333. Association for Computational Linguistics.

Weiwei Ding and Baobao Chang. 2009. Word based chinese semantic role labeling with semantic chunking. *International Journal of Computer Processing Of Languages*, 22(02n03):133–154.

Daniel Gildea and Daniel Jurafsky. 2002. Automatic labeling of semantic roles. *Computational linguistics*, 28(3):245–288.

Luheng He, Kenton Lee, Mike Lewis, and Luke Zettlemoyer. 2017. Deep semantic role labeling: What works and whats next. In *Proceedings of the Annual Meeting of the Association for Computational Linguistics*.

Sameer Pradhan, Kadri Hacioglu, Wayne Ward, James H Martin, and Daniel Jurafsky. 2005. Semantic role chunking combining complementary syntactic views. In *Proceedings of the Ninth Conference on Computational Natural Language Learning*, pages 217–220. Association for Computational Linguistics.

Vasin Punyakanok, Dan Roth, and Wen-tau Yih. 2008. The importance of syntactic parsing and inference in semantic role labeling. *Computational Linguistics*, 34(2):257–287.

Michael Roth and Mirella Lapata. 2016. Neural semantic role labeling with dependency path embeddings. *arXiv preprint arXiv:1605.07515*.

Lei Sha, Tingsong Jiang, Sujian Li, Baobao Chang, and Zhifang Sui. 2016. Capturing argument relationships for chinese semantic role labeling. In *EMNLP*, pages 2011–2016.

Honglin Sun and Daniel Jurafsky. 2004. Shallow semantic parsing of chinese. In *Proceedings of NAACL 2004*, pages 249–256.

Weiwei Sun. 2010. Improving chinese semantic role labeling with rich syntactic features. In *Proceedings of the ACL 2010 conference short papers*, pages 168–172. Association for Computational Linguistics.

Weiwei Sun, Zhifang Sui, Meng Wang, and Xin Wang. 2009. Chinese semantic role labeling with shallow parsing. In *Proceedings of the 2009 Conference on Empirical Methods in Natural Language Processing: Volume 3-Volume 3*, pages 1475–1483. Association for Computational Linguistics.

Zhen Wang, Tingsong Jiang, Baobao Chang, and Zhifang Sui. 2015. Chinese semantic role labeling with bidirectional recurrent neural networks. In *EMNLP*, pages 1626–1631.

Huijia Wu, Jiajun Zhang, and Chengqing Zong. 2016. An empirical exploration of skip connections for sequential tagging. *arXiv preprint arXiv:1610.03167*.

Deyi Xiong, Min Zhang, and Haizhou Li. 2012. Modeling the translation of predicate-argument structure for smt. In *Proceedings of the 50th Annual Meeting of the Association for Computational Linguistics: Long Papers-Volume 1*, pages 902–911. Association for Computational Linguistics.

Nianwen Xue. 2008. Labeling chinese predicates with semantic roles. *Computational linguistics*, 34(2):225–255.

Nianwen Xue and Martha Palmer. 2003. Annotating the propositions in the penn chinese treebank. In *Proceedings of the second SIGHAN workshop on Chinese language processing-Volume 17*, pages 47–54. Association for Computational Linguistics.

Nianwen Xue and Martha Palmer. 2005. Automatic semantic role labeling for chinese verbs. In *IJCAI*, volume 5, pages 1160–1165. Citeseer.

Haitong Yang, Chengqing Zong, et al. 2014. Multi-predicate semantic role labeling. In *EMNLP*, pages 363–373.

Jie Zhou and Wei Xu. 2015. End-to-end learning of semantic role labeling using recurrent neural networks. In *Proceedings of the Annual Meeting of the Association for Computational Linguistics*.

Spatial Language Understanding with Multimodal Graphs using Declarative Learning based Programming

Parisa Kordjamshidi and **Taher Rahgooy** and **Umar Manzoor**
Computer Science Department, Tulane University, New Orleans, USA
{pkordjam,trahgooy,umanzoor}@tulane.edu

Abstract

This work is on a previously formalized semantic evaluation task of spatial role labeling (SpRL) that aims at extraction of formal spatial meaning from text. Here, we report the results of initial efforts towards exploiting visual information in the form of images to help spatial language understanding. We discuss the way of designing new models in the framework of declarative learning-based programming (DeLBP). The DeLBP framework facilitates combining modalities and representing various data in a unified graph. The learning and inference models exploit the structure of the unified graph as well as the global first order domain constraints beyond the data to predict the semantics which forms a structured meaning representation of the spatial context. Continuous representations are used to relate the various elements of the graph originating from different modalities. We improved over the state-of-the-art results on SpRL.

1 Introduction

Spatial language understanding is important in many real-world applications such as geographical information systems, robotics, and navigation when the robot has a camera on the head and receives instructions about grabbing objects and finding their locations, etc. One approach towards spatial language understanding is to map the natural language to a formal spatial representation appropriate for spatial reasoning. The previous research on spatial role labeling (Kordjamshidi et al., 2010, 2017b, 2012) and ISO-Space (Pustejovsky et al., 2011, 2015) aimed at formalizing such a problem and providing machine learning solutions to find such a mapping in a data-driven way (Kordjamshidi and Moens, 2015; Kordjamshidi et al., 2011). Such extractions are made from available textual resources. However, spatial semantics are the most relevant and useful information for visualization of the language and, consequently, accompanying visual information could help disambiguation and extraction of the spatial meaning from text. Recently, there has been a large community effort to prepare new resources for combining vision and language data (Krishna et al., 2017) though not explicitly focused on formal spatial semantic representations. The current tasks are mostly image centered such as image captioning, that is, generating image descriptions (Kiros et al., 2014; Karpathy and Li, 2014), image retrieval using textual descriptions, or visual question answering (Antol et al., 2015). In this work, we consider a different problem, that is, how images can help in the extraction of a structured spatial meaning representation from text. This task has been recently proposed as a CLEF pilot task[1], the data is publicly available and the task overview will be published (Kordjamshidi et al., 2017a). Our interest in formal meaning representation distinguishes our work from other vision and language tasks and the choice of the data since our future goal is to integrate explicit qualitative spatial reasoning models into learning and spatial language understanding.

The contribution of this paper is a) we report results on combining vision and language that extend and improve the spatial role labeling state-of-the-art models, b) we model the task in the framework of declarative learning based programming and show its expressiveness in representing such complex structured output tasks. DeLBP provides the possibility of seamless integration of heteroge-

[1] http://www.cs.tulane.edu/~pkordjam/mSpRL_CLEF_lab.htm

Proceedings of the 2nd Workshop on Structured Prediction for Natural Language Processing, pages 33–43
Copenhagen, Denmark, September 7–11, 2017.

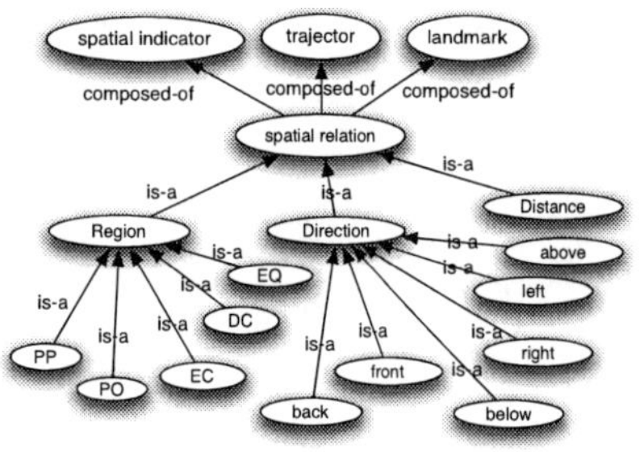

Figure 1: Given spatial ontology (Kordjamshidi and Moens, 2015)

neous data in addition to considering domain ontological and linguistic knowledge in learning and inference. To improve the state-of-the-art results in SpRL and exploiting the visual information we rely on *existing* techniques for continuous representations of image segments and text phrases, and measuring similarity to find the best alignments.

The challenging aspect of this work is that the formal representation of the textual spatial semantics is very different from the raw spatial information extracted from image segments using their geometrical relationships. To alleviate this problem the embeddings of phrases as well as the embeddings of the relations helped connecting the two modalities. This approach helped improving the state of the art results on spatial role labeling (Kordjamshidi et al., 2012) for recognizing spatial roles.

2 Problem Description

The goal is to extract spatial information from text while exploiting accompanying visual resources, that is, images. We briefly define the task which is based on a previous formalization of spatial role labeling (SpRL) (Kordjamshidi et al., 2011; Kordjamshidi and Moens, 2015). Given a piece of text, S, here a sentence, which is segmented into a number of phrases, the goal is to identify the phrases that carry spatial roles and classify them according to a given set of spatial concepts; identify the links between the roles and form spatial relations (triplets) and finally classify the spatial relations given a set of relation types. A more formal definition of the problem is given in Section 5, where we describe our computational model. The spatial concepts and relation types are depicted in Figure 1 which shows a light-weight spatial ontology. Figure 2 shows an example of an image and the related textual description. The **first level** of this task is to extract spatial roles including,

(a) **Spatial indicators (sp):** these are triggers indicating the existence of spatial information in a sentence;

(b) **Trajectors (tr):** these are the entities whose location are described;

(c) **Landmarks (lm):** these are the reference objects for describing the location of the trajectors.

In the textual description of Figure 2, the location of *kids (trajector)* has been described with respect to the *stairs (landmark)* using the preposition *on (spatial indicator)*. This is example of some spatial roles that we aim to extract from the whole text. The **second level** of this task is to extract spatial relations.

(d) **Spatial relations (sr):** these indicate a link between the three above mentioned roles $(sp.tr.lm)$, forming spatial triplets.

(e) **Relation types:** these indicate the type of relations in terms of spatial calculi formalisms. Each relation can have multiple types.

For the above example we have the triplet $spatial\_relation(kids, on, stairs)$. Recognizing the spatial relations is very challenging because there could be several spatial roles in the sentence and the model should be able to recognize the right links. The formal type of this relation could be EC that is externally connected. The previous research (Kordjamshidi and Moens, 2015) shows the extraction of triplets is the most challenging part of the task for this dataset, therefore we focus on (a)-(d) tasks in this paper. The hypothesis of this paper is that knowing the objects and their geometrical relationships in the companion image might help the inference for the extraction of roles as well as the relations from sentences. In our training dataset, the alignment between the text and image is very coarse-grained and merely the whole text is associated with the image, that is, no sentence alignment, no phrase alignment for segments, etc is available.

Each companion image I contains a number of segments each of which is related to an object and the objects spatial relationships can be described qualitatively based on their geometrical structure of the image. In this paper, we assume the image segments are given and the image object annotations are based on a given object ontology. More-

Figure 2: Image textual description:"About 20 kids in traditional clothing and hats waiting on stairs. A house and a green wall with gate in the background. A sign saying that plants can't be picked up on the right."

over, the relationships between objects in the images are assumed to be given. The spatial relationships are obtained by parsing the images and computing a number of relations based on geometrical relationships between the objects boundaries. This implies the spatial representation of the objects in the image is very different from the spatial ontology that we use to describe the spatial meaning from text; this issue makes combining information from images very challenging.

3 Declarative Modeling

To extend the SpRL task to a multimodal setting, we firstly, replicated the state-of-the-art models using the framework of declarative learning based programming (DeLBP) *Saul* (Kordjamshidi et al., 2015, 2016). The goal was to extend the previously designed configurations easily and facilitate the integration of various resources of data and knowledge into learning models. In DeLBP framework, we need to define the following building blocks for an application program,

(a) **DataModel:** Declaring a graph schema to represent the domain's concepts and their relationships. This is a first order graph called a *data-model* and can be populated with the actual data instances.

(b) **Learners:** Declaring basic learning models in terms of their inputs and outputs; where the inputs and outputs are properties of the *data-model*'s nodes.

(c) **Constraints:** Declaring constraints among output labels using first order logical expressions.

(d) **Application program:** Specifying the final end-to-end program that starts with reading the raw data into the declared *data-model* graph referred to as data population and then calls the learners and constrained learners for training, prediction and evaluation.

Each application program defines the configuration of an end-to-end model based on the abovementioned components. In the following sections we describe these components and the way they are defined for multimodal spatial role labeling.

3.1 Data Model

A graph is used to explicitly represent the structure of the data. This graph is called the *data-model* and contains *typed* nodes, edges and properties. The node types are domain's basic data structures, called *base types*. The base types are mostly preestablished in *Saul* (Kordjamshidi et al., 2016), including base types for representing documents, sentences, phrases, etc, referred to as *linguistic units*. In this work, we also have added a set of preliminary image base types in *Saul* that could be extended to facilitate working on visual data task-independently in the future. The below code shows a data model schema including nodes of linguistic units and image segments. The *typed* nodes are declared as follows:

```
val documents = node[Document]
val sentences = node[Sentence]
val tokens = node[Token]
val phrases = node[Phrase]
val pairs = node[Relation]
val images = node[Image]
val segments = node[Segement]
val segmentPairs = node[SegmentRelation]
```

('val' is a Scala keyword to define variables; documents, sentences, etc, are the programmer-defined variables; 'node' is a Saul keyword to define typed graph nodes; Document, Sentence, etc, are the NLP and other base types built-in for Saul.)

Given the base types, domain sensors can be used to populate raw data into the *data-model*. Sensors are black box functions that operate on base types and can generate instances of nodes, properties and edges. An edge that connects documents to sentences using a sensor called 'documentToSentenceMatching' is defined as:

```
val documentTosentence = edge(documents,
    sentences)
documentTosentence.addSensor(
    documentToSentenceMatching_)
```

('edge' is a Saul keyword, addSensor is a Saul function)

The properties are assigned to the graph nodes only and defined based on the existing domain property sensors. The following example receives a phrase and returns the dependency relation label of its head:

```
val headDependencyRelation = property(
    phrases){x => getDependencyRelation
    (getHeadword(x))}
```

('property' is a keyword in Saul, getDependencyRelation and getHeadword are two NLP sensors applied on words and phrases respectively.)

3.2 Learners

The learners are basically a set of classic classifiers each of which is related to a target variable in the output space. The output variables are a subset of elements represented in the ontology of Figure 1. The previous work shows the challenging element of the ontology is the extraction of spatial triplets. Therefore, in this work our goal is to improve the extraction of the roles and spatial triplets. Each classifier/learner is applied on a typed node which is defined in the *data-model*. For example, a *trajector role classifier* is applied on the `phrase` nodes and defined as follows:

```
object TrajectorRoleClassifier extends
    Learnable(phrases) {
    def label = trajectorRole
    override lazy val classifier = new
    SparseNetworkLearner
    override def feature = using(
    headDependencyRelation,...)}
```

('label' is a Saul function to define the output of the classifier, 'trajectorRole' is a name of a property in the datamodel to be predicted. 'feature' is a Saul function to define the list of properties of the datamodel to be used as input features.)

All other learners are defined similarly and they can use different types of *data-model* properties as 'feature's or as 'label'. In our proposed model, only the role and pair classifiers are used and triplets of relations are generated based on the results of the pair classifiers afterwards.

3.2.1 Role and Relation Properties

Spatial Roles are applied on phrases and most of the features are used based on the previous works (Kordjamshidi and Moens, 2015), however the previous work on this data is mostly token-based; we have extended the features to phrase-based and added some more features. We use linguistically motivated features such as lexical form of the words in the phrases, lemmas, pos-tags, dependency relations, subcategorization, etc. These features are used sometimes based on the headword of the phrases and sometimes by concatenation of the same features for all the tokens in a phrase. The relations are, in-fact, a pair of phrases and the pair features are based on the features of the phrases. The relational features between two phrases include their path, distance, before/after information. In addition to the previously used features, here, we add phrase and image embeddings described in the next section. The details of the linguistic features are omitted due to the lack of space and since the code is publicly available.

3.2.2 Image and Text Embeddings

Using continuous representations has several advantages in our models. One important aspect is compensating for the lack of lexical information due to the lack of training data for this problem. Another aspect is the mapping between image segments and the phrases occurring in the textual descriptions and establishing a connection between the two modalities. The experiments show these components improve the generalization capability of our trained models. Since our dataset is very small, our best embeddings were the commonly used word2vec (Pennington et al., 2014) model trained over google's gigaword+wikipedia corpora.

Text Embeddings. We generate the embeddings for candidate roles. More specifically, for each phrase we find its syntactic head and then we use the vector representation of the syntactic head as a feature of the phrase. This is added to the rest of linguistically motivated features.

Image Embeddings. For the image side we rely on a number of assumptions given the type of image corpora available for our task. As mentioned in Section 1, the input images are assumed to be segmented and the segments have been labeled according to a given ontology of concepts. For example, the ontology for a specific object like *Bush* can be `entity->landscape-nature->vegetation->trees->bush`. Given the image segments, the spatial relations between segments are automatically extracted in a pairwise exhaustive manner using the geometrical properties of the segments (Escalante et al., 2010). These relations are limited to relationships such as besides, disjoint, below, above, x-aligned, and y-aligned. In this work, we employed the pre-processed images that were publicly available[2]. Since the segment label ontology is independent from the textual descriptions, finding the alignment between the segments and the words/phrases in the text is very challenging. To alleviate this problem, we exploit the embeddings of the image segment labels using the same representations that is used for words in the text. We measure the similarity between the segment label embeddings and word embeddings to help the fine-grained alignments between the image segments and text phrases. To clarify, we tried the following variations: we compute the word embeddings of image segment labels and words in the text candidate phrases, then we find the most similar object in the image to each candidate phrase. We use the embedding of the most similar object as a feature of the phrase. Another variation that we tried is to exploit the embeddings of the image segment ontologies. The vector representation of each segment label is computed by averaging over the representation of all the ontological concepts related to that segment.

3.3 Global Constraints

The key point of considering global correlations in our extraction model is formalizing a number of global constraints and exploiting those in learning and inference. The constraints are declared using first order logical expressions, for example, the constraint, "if there exists a trajector or a landmark in the sentence then an indicator should also exist in the sentence" , we call it integrity constraint and it is expressed as follows:

```
((sentences(s)~>phraseEdge)._exists{x:
    Phrase=>(TrajectorRoleClassifier on
    x is "Trajector") or (
    LandmarkRoleClassifier on x is "
    Landmark"}))==>((sentences(s)~>
    phraseEdge)._exists{y:Phrase=>
    IndicatorRoleClassifier on y is "
    Indicator"})
```

The domain knowledge is inspired from this work (Kordjamshidi and Moens, 2015).[3] The first order constraints are automatically converted to linear algebraic constraints for our underlying computational models.

4 Application program

Using the building blocks of a DeLBP including a *data-model*, *learners* and *constraints*, we are able to design various end-to-end configurations for learning and inference. The first step for an application program is to populate the annotated corpus in the graph schema, that is, our declared *data-model*. To simplify the procedure of populating the graph with linguistic annotations, we have established a generic XML reader that is able to read the annotated corpora from XML into the Saul *data-model* and provide us a populated graph. The nodes related to the linguistic units (i.e. sentence, phrase, etc) are populated with the annotations as their properties. The population can be done in various ways, for example, `SpRLDatamodel.documents.populate (xmlReader.documentList())` reads the content of DOCUMENT tag or its pre-defined[4] equivalent into `documents` nodes in the *data-model*. Populating documents can lead to populating all other types of nodes such as sentences, tokens, etc if the necessary sensors and edges are specified beforehand. Saul functions and *data-model* primitives can be used to make graph traversal queries to access any information that we need from either image or text for candidate selection, feature extraction.

The feature extraction includes segmentation of the text and candidate generation for roles and pair relations. Not all tokens are candidates for playing trajector roles, most certainly verbs will not play this role. After populating the data into the graph we program the training strategy. We have the possibility of training for each concept independently, that is, each declared classifier can call the `learn` , for example, `trajectorClassifier.learn()`. However, the independently trained classifiers can exploit the global constraints like the one we defined in Section 3.3 and be involved in a global inference jointly with other role and relation classifiers. Such a model is referred to as L+I (Punyakanok et al., 2008). Moreover, the parameters of the declared classifiers can be trained jointly and for this purpose we need to call `joinTrain` and pass the list of classifiers and the constraints to be used together. We use L+I models in this paper due to the efficiency of the training.

5 Computational Model

The problem we address in this paper is formulated as a structured prediction problem as the out-

[2]http://www.imageclef.org/photodata

[3]constraints code is available on GitHub.

[4]The programmer is able to specify the tags that are related to the base types before reading the xml.

put contains a number of spatial roles and relationships that obey some global constraints. In learning models for structured output prediction, given a set of N input-output pairs of training examples $E = \{(x^i, y^i) \in \mathcal{X} \times \mathcal{Y} : i = 1..N\}$, we learn an objective function $g(x, y; W)$ which is a linear *discriminant* function defined over the combined feature representation of the inputs and outputs denoted by $f(x, y)$ (Ioannis Tsochantaridis and Altun, 2006):

$$g(x, y; W) = \langle W, f(x, y) \rangle. \quad (1)$$

W denotes a weight vector and $\langle , \rangle$ denotes a dot product between two vectors. A popular discriminative training approach is to minimize the following convex upper bound of the loss function over the training data:

$$l(W) = \sum_{i=1}^{N} \max_{y \in \mathcal{Y}} (g(x^i, y; W) - g(x^i, y^i; W) \quad + \Delta(y^i, y)),$$

the inner maximization is called loss-augmented inference and finds the so called most violated constraints/outputs (y) per training example. This is the base of inference-based-training models (IBT). However, the inference over structures can be limited to the prediction time which is known as learning plus inference (L+I) models. L+I uses the independently trained models (this is known as piece-wise training as well (Sutton and McCallum, 2009)) and has shown to be very efficient and competitive compared to IBT models in various tasks (Punyakanok et al., 2005). Given this general formalization of the problem we can easily consider both configurations of L+I and IBT using a declarative representation of our inference problem as briefly discussed in Section 4. We define our structured model in terms of first order constraints and classifiers.

Here in *Saul*'s generic setting, inputs $\boldsymbol{x}$ and outputs $\boldsymbol{y}$ are sub-graphs of the *data-model* and each learning model can use parts and substructures of this graph. In other words, $\boldsymbol{x}$ is a set of nodes $\{x_1, \ldots, x_K\}$ and each node has a *type* p. Each $x_k \in \boldsymbol{x}$ is described by a set of properties; this set of properties will be converted to a feature vector ϕ_p. Given the multimodal setting of our problem, x_i 's can represent segments of an image or various linguistic units of a text, such as a phrase (*atomic node*) or a pair of phrases (*composed node*), and each type is described by its own properties (e.g. a phrase by its headword, the pair by the distance of the two headwords, an image segment by the vector representation of its concept). We refer to the text-related nodes and image-related nodes differently as x_T and x_I, respectively. The goal is to map this pair to a set of spatial objects and spatial relationships, that is $f : (x_T, x_I) \mapsto y$.

The output $\boldsymbol{y}$ is represented by a set of *labels* $\boldsymbol{l} = \{l_1, \ldots, l_P\}$ each of which is a *property* of a node. The labels can have semantic relationships. In our model the set of labels is $l = \{tr, lm, sp, sp.tr, sp.lm, sp.tr.lm\}$. Note that these labels are applied merely to the parts of the text, tr, lm and sp are applied on the phrase of a sentence, $sp.tr$ and $sp.lm$ are applied on pairs of phrases in the sentence, and finally $sp.tr.lm$ is applied on triplets of phrases. According to the terminology used in (Kordjamshidi and Moens, 2015), the labels of atomic components of the text (here phrases) are referred to as *single-labels* and the labels that are applied to composed components of the input such as pairs or triplets are referred to as *linked-labels*. These labels help to represent y with a set of indicator functions that indicate which *segments* of the sentence play a specific spatial role and which are involved in relations. The labels are defined with a graph query that extracts a property from the *data-model*. The $l_p(x_k)$ or shorter l_{pk} denotes an indicator function indicating whether component x_k has the label l_p. For example, $sp(on)$ shows whether on plays a spatial role and $sp.tr(on, kids)$ shows whether $kids$ is a trajector of on. As expected, the form of the output is dependent on the input since we are dealing with a structured output prediction problem. In our problem setting the spatial roles and relations are still assigned to the components of the text and the connections, similarities and embeddings from image are used as additional information for improving the extractions from text.

The main objective g is written in terms of the instantiations of the feature functions, labels and their related blocks of weights $\boldsymbol{w}_p$ in $\boldsymbol{w} = [\boldsymbol{w}_1, \boldsymbol{w}_2, \ldots, \boldsymbol{w}_P]$,

$$\begin{aligned} g(\boldsymbol{x}, \boldsymbol{y}; \boldsymbol{w}) &= \sum_{l_p \in \boldsymbol{l}} \sum_{x_k \in C_{l_p}} \langle \boldsymbol{w}_p, f_p(x_k, l_p) \rangle \quad (2) \\ &= \sum_{l_p \in \boldsymbol{l}} \sum_{x_k \in C_{l_p}} \langle \boldsymbol{w}_p, \phi_p(x_k) \rangle \, l_{pk} \\ &= \sum_{l_p \in \boldsymbol{l}} \left\langle \boldsymbol{w}_p, \sum_{x_k \in C_{l_p}} (\phi_p(x_k) l_{pk}) \right\rangle, \end{aligned}$$

where $f_p(\boldsymbol{x}_k, l_p)$ are the local joint feature vector for each candidate $\boldsymbol{x}_k$. This feature vector is computed by scalar multiplication of the input feature vector of $\boldsymbol{x}_k$ (i.e. $\phi_p(\boldsymbol{x}_k)$), and the output label l_{pk}.

Given this objective, we can view the inference task as a *combinatorial constrained optimization* given the polynomial g which is written in terms of labels, subject to the constraints that describe the relationships between the labels (either single or linked labels). For example, the *is-a* relationships can be defined as the following constraint, $(l(\boldsymbol{x}_c)\ is\ 1) \Rightarrow (l'(x_c)\ is\ 1)$, where l and l' are two distinct labels that are applicable on the node with the same type of $\boldsymbol{x}_c$. These constraints are added as a part of *Saul*'s objective, so we have the following objective form, which is in fact a constrained conditional model (Chang et al., 2012), $g = \langle \boldsymbol{w}, f(\boldsymbol{x}, \boldsymbol{y})\rangle - \langle \rho, c(\boldsymbol{x}, \boldsymbol{y})\rangle$, where c is the constraint function and ρ is the vector of penalties for violating each constraint. This representation corresponds to an integer linear program, and thus can be used to encode any MAP problem. Specifically, the g function is written as the sum of local joint feature functions which are the counterparts of the probabilistic factors:

$$g(\boldsymbol{x}, \boldsymbol{y}; \boldsymbol{w}) = \sum_{l_p \in \boldsymbol{l}} \sum_{\boldsymbol{x}_k \in \{\tau\}} \langle \boldsymbol{w}_p, f_p(\boldsymbol{x}_k, l_{pk})\rangle + \sum_{m=1}^{|C|} \rho_m c_m(\boldsymbol{x}, \boldsymbol{y}), \tag{3}$$

where C is a set of global constraints that can hold among various types of nodes. g can represent a general scoring function rather than the one corresponding to the likelihood of an assignment. Note that this objective is automatically generated based on the high level specifications of learners and constraints as described in Section 3.

6 Experimental Results

In this section, we experimentally show the influence of our new features, constraints, phrase embeddings and image embeddings and compare them with the previous research.

Data. We use the SemEval-2012 shared tasks data (Kordjamshidi et al., 2012) that consists of textual descriptions of 613 images originally selected from the IAPR TC-12 dataset (Grubinger et al., 2006), provided by the *CLEF* organization. In the previous works only the text part of this data has been used in various shared task settings (Kordjamshidi et al., 2012; Oleksandr Kolomiyets and Bethard, 2013; Pustejovsky et al., 2015) and with a variation in the annotation schemes. This data includes about 1213 sentence containing 20,095 words with 1706 annotated relations. We preferred this data compared to more recent related corpora (Pustejovsky et al., 2015; Oleksandr Kolomiyets and Bethard, 2013) for two main reasons. First is the availability of the aligned images and the second is the static nature of the most spatial descriptions.

Implementation. As mentioned before, we used *Saul* (Kordjamshidi et al., 2015, 2016) framework that allows flexible relational feature extraction as well as declarative formulation of the global inference. We extend *Saul*'s basic data structures and sensors to be able to work with multimodal data and to populate raw as well as annotated text easily into a *Saul* multimodal *data-model*. The code is available in Github.[5] We face the following challenges when solving this problem: the training data is very small; the annotation schemes for the text and images are very different and they have been annotated independently; the image annotations regarding the spatial relations include very naively generated exhaustively pairwise relations which are not very relevant to what human describes by viewing the images. We try to address these challenges by feature engineering, exploiting global constraints and using continuous representations for text and image segments. We report the results of the following models in Table 1.

BM: This is our baseline model built with extensive feature engineering as described in Section 3.2.1. We train independent classifiers for the roles and relations classification in this model;

BM+C: This is the BM that uses global constraints to impose, for example, the integrity and consistency of the assignments of the roles and relation labels at the sentence level.

BM+C+E: To deal with the lack of lexical information, the features of roles and relations are augmented by w2vec word embeddings, the results of this model without using constraints (BM+E) are reported too;

BM+E+I+C: In this model in addition to text embeddings, we augment the text phrase fea-

[5] `https://github.com/HetML/SpRL`

	Trajector			Landmark			Spatial indicator			Spatial triplet		
	Pr	R	F1	Pr	R	F1	Pr	R	F1	Pr	R	F1
BM	56.72	69.57	62.49	72.97	86.21	79.05	94.76	97.74	96.22	75.18	45.47	56.67
BM+C	65.56	69.91	67.66	77.74	87.78	82.46	94.83	96.86	95.83	75.21	48.46	58.94
BM+E	55.87	77.35	64.88	71.47	89.18	79.35	94.76	97.74	96.22	66.50	57.30	61.56
BM+E+C	64.40	76.77	70.04	76.99	89.35	82.71	94.85	97.48	96.15	68.34	57.93	**62.71**
BM+E+I	56.53	79.29	66.00	71.78	87.44	78.84	94.76	97.74	**96.22**	64.12	57.08	60.39
BM+E+I+C	64.49	77.92	**70.57**	77.66	89.18	**83.02**	94.87	97.61	96.22	66.46	57.61	61.72
BM+E+C-10f	78.49	77.67	78.03	86.43	88.93	87.62	91.70	94.71	93.17	80.85	60.23	68.95
SOP2015-10f	-	-	-	-	-	-	90.5	84	86.9	67.3	57.3	61.7
SemEval-2012	78.2	64.6	70.7	89.4	68.0	77.2	94.0	73.2	82.3	61.0	54.0	57.3

Table 1: Experimental results on SemEval-2012 data including images. BM: Baseline Model, C: Constraints, E: Text Embeddings, I: Image Embeddings.

tures with the embeddings of the most similar image segments. The version without constraints is denoted as BM+E+I.

SemEval-2012: This model is the best performing model of SemEval-2012 (Roberts and Harabagiu, 2012). It generates the candidate triplets and classifies them as spatial/not-spatial. It does an extensive feature extraction for the triplets. The roles then are simply inferred from the relations. The results are reported with the same train/test split.

SOP2015-10f: This model is an structured output prediction model that does a global inference on the whole ontology including the prediction of relations and relation types (Kordjamshidi and Moens, 2015).

The experimental results in Table 1 show that adding constraints to our baseline and other model variations consistently improves the classification of trajectors and landmarks dramatically although it slightly decreases the F1 of spatial indicators in some cases. Adding word embeddings (BM+C+E) shows a significant improvement on roles and spatial relations. The results on BM+E+I+C show that image embeddings improves trajectors and landmarks compared to BM+E+C, though the results of triples are slightly dropped (62.71 $\rightarrow$ 61.72).

Our results exceed the state of the art models reported in SemEval-2012 (Kordjamshidi et al., 2012). The SemEval-2012 best model uses same train/test split as ours (Roberts and Harabagiu, 2012). The results of the best performing model in (Kordjamshidi and Moens, 2015), SOP2015-10f, are lower than our best model in this work. Although that model uses structured training but here the embeddings make a significant improvement. While SOP2015-10f performance results on triples, spatial indicators, pairs of trajector and landmarks with indicators have been reported, there is no reports on trajecotrs and landmarks prediction accuracy as designated independent roles –those are left empty in the table. There are some differences in our evaluation and the previous systems evaluations.The SOP2015-10f is evaluated by 10-fold cross validation rather than the train/test split. To be able to compare, we report the 10-fold cross validation results of our best model BM+E+C and refer to it as BM+E+C-10f in Table 1 which is outperforming other models. Note that the folds are chosen randomly and might be different from the previous evaluation setting. Another difference is that our evaluation is done phrase-based and overlapping phrases are counted as true predictions. The SemEval-2012 and SOP2015-10f models operate on classifying tokens/words which are the headwords of the annotated roles. However, our identified phrases cover the headwords of role (trajectors and landmarks) phrases with 100% and for spatial indicators 98% which keeps the comparisons fair yet.

Our results exceed the stat-of-the-art models significantly. Both word and image embeddings help expanding our semantic dimensions for spatial objects but interestingly the spatial indicators can not be improved using embeddings. Since the indicators are mostly prepositions, it seems capturing the semantic dimensions of prepositions using continuous vectors is harder than other lexical categories such as nouns and verbs. This is even worse when we use images since the terminology of the relations in the images is very different from the way the relations are expressed in the language using prepositions. Though the improvement on objects can improve the relations but it will be interesting to investigate how the semantics of the relations can be captured using richer representations for spatial prepositions. A possible direction for our work could have been to train deep models that map the images to the formal semantic representations of the text's content, however for training such models using only 2013 sentences related to about 600 images will not be feasible. The existing large corpora which contain image and text, do not contain formal semantic annotation with the textual description. Dealing with this problems remains as our future work.

7 Related Research

This work can be related to many research works from various perspectives. However, for the sake of both clarity and conciseness, we limit our exploration in this section to two research directions. First body of related work is about the specific SpRL task that we are solving. This direction is aiming at obtaining a generic formal spatial meaning representation from text. The second body of the work is about combining vision and language which itself has a large research community around it recently and has turned to a hot topic.

Several research efforts in the past few years aimed at defining a framework for the extraction of spatial information form natural language. These efforts start from defining linguistic annotation schemes (Pustejovsky and Moszkowicz, 2008; Kordjamshidi et al., 2010; Pustejovsky and Moszkowicz, 2012; jeet Mani, 2009), annotating data and defining tasks (Kordjamshidi et al., 2012; Oleksandr Kolomiyets and Bethard, 2013; Pustejovsky et al., 2015) to operate on the annotated corpora and learn extraction models. However, there exists, yet, a large gap between the current models and the ones that can perform reasonably well in practice for real world applications in various domains. Though we follow that line of work, we aim at exploiting the visual data in improving spatial extraction models. We exploit the visual information accompanying the text which is mostly available nowadays. We aim at text understanding while assuming that the text highlights the most important information that might be confirmed by the image. Our goal is to use the image to recognize and disambiguate the spatial information from text.

Our work is very related to the research done by computer vision community and in the intersection of vision and language. There are many progressive research works on generating image captions (Karpathy and Li, 2014), retrieving images and visual question answering (Antol et al., 2015). However the center of attention has been understanding images. Here, our aim is to exploit the images for text understanding.This task is as challenging as the former ones or even more challenging because among the many possible objects and relationships in the image a very small subset of those are important and have been expressed in the text. Therefore the available visual corpora are not exactly the type of the data that can be used to train supervised models for our task though it could provide some indirect supervision particularly for having a unified semantic representation of spatial objects (Ludwig et al., 2016).

This work can be improved by exploiting external models and corpora (Pustejovsky and Yocum, 2014) but this will remain for our future investigation. Our task can benefit from the research performed on reference resolution that targets identifying the objects in the image that are mentioned in the text (Schlangen et al., 2016). Having a high-quality alignment by training explicit models for resolving references should help recognizing the spatial objects mentioned in the text and the type of spatial relations according to the image. Explicit reference resolution between modalities in dialogue systems are also inspiring (Fang et al., 2014). In the mentioned reference a graph representation of the scene is gradually made by machine based on the grasped static visual information and the representation is corrected and completed dynamically as the dialogue between the machine and human is going on. However, in this work there is no learning component and there is no spatially annotated data to be used for our goal of formal spatial meaning representation for a generic text.

In this work we take a small step and investigate the ways to integrate information from both modalities for our textual extraction target. Our results are compared to the previous work (Kordjamshidi and Moens, 2015) that exploit the text part of the same spatially annotated corpora and improve the results when exploiting the accompanying images.

8 Conclusion

In this paper, we deal with the problem of spatial role labeling which targets at mapping natural language text to a formal spatial meaning representation. We use the information from accompanying segmented images to improve the spatial role extractions. Although, there are many recent research on combining vision and language, none of them consider obtaining a formal spatial meaning representation as a target while we do and our approach will be helpful for adding explicit reasoning component to the learning models in the future. We manifest the expressivity of declarative learning based programming paradigm for designing global models for this task. We put both the image and text related to a scene in a unified *datamodel* graph and use them as structured learning examples. We extract features by traversing the graph and using the continuous representations to connect the image segment nodes to the nodes related to the text phrases. We exploit the continuous representation to align the similar concepts in the two modalities. We exploit global first order constraints for global inference over roles and relations. Our models improve the state of the art results on previous spatial role labeling models.

References

Stanislaw Antol, Aishwarya Agrawal, Jiasen Lu, Margaret Mitchell, Dhruv Batra, C. Lawrence Zitnick, and Devi Parikh. 2015. VQA: Visual Question Answering. In *International Conference on Computer Vision (ICCV)*.

Ming-Wei Chang, Lev Ratinov, and Dan Roth. 2012. Structured learning with constrained conditional models. *Machine Learning* 88(3):399–431.

Hugo Jair Escalante, Carlos A. Hernndez, Jesus A. Gonzalez, A. Lpez-Lpez, Manuel Montes, Eduardo F. Morales, L. Enrique Sucar, Luis Villaseor, and Michael Grubinger. 2010. The segmented and annotated {IAPR} tc-12 benchmark. *Computer Vision and Image Understanding* 114(4):419 – 428. Special issue on Image and Video Retrieval Evaluation. https://doi.org/http://doi.org/10.1016/j.cviu.2009.03.008.

Rui Fang, Malcolm Doering, and Joyce Y. Chai. 2014. Collaborative models for referring expression generation in situated dialogue. In *Proceedings of the Twenty-Eighth AAAI Conference on Artificial Intelligence*. AAAI Press, AAAI'14, pages 1544–1550.

Michael Grubinger, Paul D. Clough, Henning Müller, and Thomas Deselaers. 2006. The IAPR benchmark: a new evaluation resource for visual information systems. In *Proceedings of the International Conference on Language Resources and Evaluation (LREC)*. pages 13–23.

Thorsten Joachims Thomas Hofmann Ioannis Tsochantaridis and Yasemin Altun. 2006. Large margin methods for structured and interdependent output variables. *Journal of Machine Learning Research* 6(2):1453–1484.

jeet Mani. 2009. SpatialML: annotation scheme for marking spatial expression in natural language. Technical Report Version 3.0, The MITRE Corporation.

Andrej Karpathy and Fei-Fei Li. 2014. Deep visual-semantic alignments for generating image descriptions. *CoRR* abs/1412.2306.

Ryan Kiros, Ruslan Salakhutdinov, and Richard S. Zemel. 2014. Unifying visual-semantic embeddings with multimodal neural language models. *CoRR* abs/1411.2539.

Parisa Kordjamshidi, Steven Bethard, and Marie-Francine Moens. 2012. SemEval-2012 task 3: Spatial role labeling. In *Proceedings of the First Joint Conference on Lexical and Computational Semantics: Proceedings of the Sixth International Workshop on Semantic Evaluation (SemEval)*. volume 2, pages 365–373.

Parisa Kordjamshidi, Daniel Khashabi, Christos Christodoulopoulos, Bhargav Mangipudi, Sameer Singh, and Dan Roth. 2016. Better call saul: Flexible programming for learning and inference in nlp. In *Proc. of the International Conference on Computational Linguistics (COLING)*.

Parisa Kordjamshidi and Marie-Francine Moens. 2015. Global machine learning for spatial ontology population. *Web Semant.* 30(C):3–21. https://doi.org/10.1016/j.websem.2014.06.001.

Parisa Kordjamshidi, Taher Rahgooy, Marie-Francine Moens, James Pustejovsky, Umar Manzoor, and Kirk Roberts. 2017a. CLEF 2017: Multimodal Spatial Role Labeling (mSpRL) Task Overview. In Julio Gonzalo Liadh Kelly Lorraine Goeuriot Thomas Mandl Linda Cappellato Nicola Ferro Gareth J. F. Jones, Samus Lawless, editor, *Experimental IR Meets Multilinguality, Multimodality, and Interaction 8th International Conference of the CLEF Association, CLEF 2017, Dublin, Ireland, September 11-14, 2017, Proceedings*. Springer, volume 10456 of *LNCS*.

Parisa Kordjamshidi, Martijn van Otterlo, and Marie-Francine Moens. 2010. Spatial role labeling: task definition and annotation scheme. In Nicoletta Calzolari, Choukri Khalid, and Maegaard Bente, editors, *Proceedings of the Seventh Conference on International Language Resources and Evaluation (LREC'10)*. pages 413–420.

Parisa Kordjamshidi, Martijn van Otterlo, and Marie-Francine Moens. 2011. Spatial role labeling: towards extraction of spatial relations from natural language. *ACM - Transactions on Speech and Language Processing* 8:1–36.

Parisa Kordjamshidi, Martijn van Otterlo, and Marie-Francine Moens. 2017b. Spatial role labeling annotation scheme. In N. Ide James Pustejovsky, editor, *Handbook of Linguistic Annotation*, Springer Verlag.

Parisa Kordjamshidi, Hao Wu, and Dan Roth. 2015. Saul: Towards declarative learning based programming. In *Proc. of the International Joint Conference on Artificial Intelligence (IJCAI)*.

Ranjay Krishna, Yuke Zhu, Oliver Groth, Justin Johnson, Kenji Hata, Joshua Kravitz, Stephanie Chen, Yannis Kalantidis, Li-Jia Li, David A. Shamma, Michael S. Bernstein, and Fei-Fei Li. 2017. Visual genome: Connecting language and vision using crowdsourced dense image annotations. *International Journal of Computer Vision* .

Oswaldo Ludwig, Xiao Liu, Parisa Kordjamshidi, and Marie-Francine Moens. 2016. Deep embedding for spatial role labeling. *CoRR* abs/1603.08474.

Parisa Kordjamshidi Marie-Francine Moens Oleksandr Kolomiyets and Steven Bethard. 2013. Semeval-2013 task 3: Spatial role labeling. In *Second Joint Conference on Lexical and Computational Semantics (*SEM), Volume 2: Proceedings of the Seventh International Workshop on Semantic Evaluation (SemEval 2013)*. Atlanta, Georgia, USA, pages 255–262.

Jeffrey Pennington, Richard Socher, and Christopher D Manning. 2014. Glove: Global vectors for word representation. In *EMNLP*. volume 14, pages 1532–1543.

Vasin Punyakanok, Dan Roth, and W. Yih. 2008. The importance of syntactic parsing and inference in semantic role labeling. *Computational Linguistics* 34(2).

Vasin Punyakanok, Dan Roth, W. Tau Yih, and D. Zimak. 2005. Learning and inference over constrained output. In *IJCAI'05*. pages 1124–1129.

James Pustejovsky, Parisa Kordjamshidi, Marie-Francine Moens, Aaron Levine, Seth Dworman, and Zachary Yocum. 2015. SemEval-2015 task 8: SpaceEval. In *Proceedings of the 9th International Workshop on Semantic Evaluation (SemEval 2015), 9th international workshop on semantic evaluation (SemEval 2015), Denver, Colorado, 4-5 June 2015*. ACL, pages 884–894.

James Pustejovsky, J. Moszkowicz, and M. Verhagen. 2011. ISO-Space: The annotation of spatial information in language. In *ACL-ISO International Workshop on Semantic Annotation (ISA'6)*.

James Pustejovsky and J. L. Moszkowicz. 2008. Integrating motion predicate classes with spatial and temporal annotations. In Donia Scott and Hans Uszkoreit, editors, *COLING 2008: Companion volume D, Posters and Demonstrations*. pages 95–98.

James Pustejovsky and J. L. Moszkowicz. 2012. The role of model testing in standards development: The case of ISO-space. In *Proceedings of LREC'12*. European Language Resources Association (ELRA), pages 3060–3063.

James Pustejovsky and Zachary Yocum. 2014. Image annotation with iso-space: Distinguishing content from structure. In Nicoletta Calzolari (Conference Chair), Khalid Choukri, Thierry Declerck, Hrafn Loftsson, Bente Maegaard, Joseph Mariani, Asuncion Moreno, Jan Odijk, and Stelios Piperidis, editors, *Proceedings of the Ninth International Conference on Language Resources and Evaluation (LREC'14)*. European Language Resources Association (ELRA), Reykjavik, Iceland.

Kirk Roberts and S.M. Harabagiu. 2012. UTD-SpRL: A joint approach to spatial role labeling. In **SEM 2012: The First Joint Conference on Lexical and Computational Semantics, Volume 2: Proceedings of the Sixth International Workshop on Semantic Evaluation (SemEval'12)*. pages 419–424.

David Schlangen, Sina Zarrie, and Casey Kennington. 2016. Resolving References to Objects in Photographs using the Words-As-Classifiers Model. In *Proceedings of the 54th Annual Meeting of the Association for Computational Linguistics (ACL 2016)*.

Charles Sutton and Andrew McCallum. 2009. Piecewise training for structured prediction. *Machine Learning* 77:165–194. https://doi.org/10.1007/s10994-009-5112-z.

Boosting Information Extraction Systems with Character-level Neural Networks and Free Noisy Supervision

Philipp Meerkamp
Bloomberg LP
731 Lexington Avenue
New York, NY 10022
USA
pmeerkamp@bloomberg.net

Zhengyi Zhou
AT&T Labs Research
33 Thomas Street
New York, NY 10007
USA
zzhou@research.att.com

Abstract

We present an architecture to boost the precision of existing information extraction systems. This is achieved by augmenting the existing parser, which may be constraint-based or hybrid statistical, with a character-level neural network. Our architecture combines the ability of constraint-based or hybrid extraction systems to easily incorporate domain knowledge with the ability of deep neural networks to leverage large amounts of data to learn complex features. The network is trained using a measure of consistency between extracted data and existing databases as a form of cheap, noisy supervision. Our architecture does not require large scale manual annotation or a system rewrite. It has led to large precision improvements over an existing, highly-tuned production information extraction system used at Bloomberg LP for financial language text.

1 Introduction

1.1 Information extraction in finance

Unstructured textual data is abundant in the financial domain (see Figure 1). This type of text is usually not in a format that lends itself to immediate processing. Hence, information extraction is an essential step in many business applications that wish to use the financial text data. Examples of such business applications include creating time series databases for macroeconomic forecasting, or real-time extraction of time series data to inform algorithmic trading strategies. For example, consider extracting data from Figure 1 into numerical relations of the form
ts_tick_abs (TS symbol, numerical value),

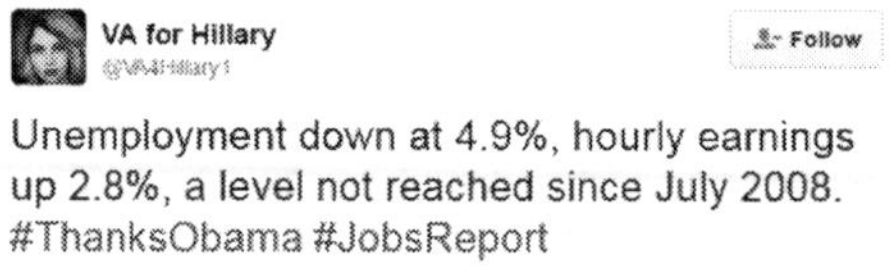

Figure 1: Tweet containing financial data.

e.g. *ts_tick_abs (US_Unemployment, 4.9%)*, or
ts_tick_rel (TS symbol, change in num. value),
e.g. *ts_tick_abs (US_Hourly_Earnings, 2.8%)*.
For these business applications, the extraction needs to be fast, accurate, and low-cost.

There are several challenges to extracting information from financial language text.

- Financial text can be very ambiguous. Language in the financial domain often trades grammatical correctness for brevity. A multitude of numeric tokens need to be disambiguated into entities such as prices, rates, percentage changes, quantities, dates, times, and others. Finally, many words could be company names, stock symbols, domain-specific terms, or have entirely different meanings.

- Large-scale annotated data with ground truths is typically not available. Domain expert manual annotations are expensive and limited in scale. This is especially a problem because the size of the problem domain is large, with many types of financial instruments, language conventions, and text formats.

These two challenges lead to a high risk of extracting false positives.

Bloomberg has mature information extraction systems for financial language text, that are the result of nearly a decade of efforts. When improving

Proceedings of the 2nd Workshop on Structured Prediction for Natural Language Processing, pages 44–51
Copenhagen, Denmark, September 7–11, 2017.

upon such large industrial extraction systems, it is invaluable if the proposed improvement does not require a complete system rewrite.

The existing extraction systems leverage both constraint-based and statistical methods. Constraint-based methods can effectively incorporate domain knowledge (e.g. unemployment numbers cannot be negative numbers, while changes in unemployment numbers *can* be negative). These constraints can be complex, and may involve multiple entities within an extraction candidate. Adding a single constraint can in many cases vastly improve the system's accuracy. In a purely statistical system, achieving the equivalent behavior would require large amounts of labeled training data.

This existing systems generate extractions with high recall, and in this work, we propose to boost the precision of the existing systems using a deep neural network.

1.2 Our contribution

We present an information extraction architecture that boosts the precision of an existing parser using a deep neural network. The architecture gains the neural network's ability to leverage large amounts of data to learn complex features specific to the application at hand. At the same time, the existing parser may leverage constraints to easily incorporate domain knowledge. Our method uses potentially noisy but cheaply available source of supervision, e.g. via consistency checks of extracted data against existing databases (e.g. an extraction *ts_tick_abs (US_Unemployment, 49%)* would be implausible given recent US employment history), or via human interaction (e.g., clicks on online advertisements).

Our extraction system has two main advantages

- We improve the existing extraction systems cheaply using large amounts of free noisy labels, without the need for manual annotation. This is particularly valuable in large application domains, where manual annotations covering the entire domain would be prohibitively expensive.

- Our method leverages existing codebases fully, and requires no system rewrite. This is critical in large industrial extraction systems, where a rewrite would take many man-years. Even for new systems, the decoupling of candidate-generation and the neural network offers advantages: the candidate-generating parser can easily enforce constraints that would be difficult to incorporate in a system relying entirely on neural networks.

We are not aware of alternative approaches that achieve the above: purely neural network or purely statistical approaches require substantial amounts of human annotation, while our method does not. Constraint-based or hybrid statistical approaches are competitors to the existing extraction systems rather than our work; our work could also be used to boost the precision of other state-of-the-art constraint or hybrid methods. We believe that our approach, with small modifications, can be applied to extraction systems in many other applications.

Compared to the existing, client-serving extraction engine, our system reduced the number of false positive extractions by $> 90\%$. Our system constituted a substantial improvement and is being deployed to production.

We review some related work in Section 1.3. Section 2 details the design, training, and method supervision of our system. We present results in Section 3 and conclude with some discussions in Section 4.

1.3 Related Work

Deep neural networks have been applied to several problems in natural language processing recently. Mikolov introduced the recurrent network language model (Kombrink et al., 2011), which can for instance consume the beginning of a sentence word by word, encoding the sentence in its state vector, and predict a likely continuation of the sentence. Long Short Term Memory (LSTM) architectures (Gehrs, 2001; Hochreiter and Schmidhuber, 1997) have resulted in large improvements in machine translation (Sutskever et al., 2014). There is a growing literature of LSTMs and deep convolutional architectures being used for text classification (e.g. (Zhang et al., 2015; Kim, 2014; dos Santos and Gatti, 2014)) and language modeling problems (Kim et al., 2016; Karpathy, 2015).

Several studies have considered using deep neural networks for information extraction problems. Socher et al introduce compositional vector grammars, which combine probabilistic context free grammars with a recursive neural network (2013). Nguyen et al use convolutional neural networks

(CNN) and recurrent neural networks with word- and entity-position-embeddings for relation extraction and event detection (Nguyen et al., 2016; Nguyen and Grishman, 2015). Zhou and Xu use a bidirectional (Schuster and Paliwal, 1997) word-level LSTM combined with a conditional random field (CRF) (Lafferty et al., 2001) for semantic role labeling (2015). In some cases, providing a neural network character-level rather than word-level input can be beneficial. Chiu and Nichols use a bidirectional LSTM-CNN with character embeddings for named entity recognition (2015), and Ballesteros et al found that character-level LSTM improve dependency parsing accuracy in many languages, relative to word-level approaches (2015). Recently, Miwa and Bansal presented an end-to-end LSTM-based architecture for relation extraction, achieving state-of-the-art results on SemEval-2010 Task 8 (2016).

While much of the recent work on information extraction focuses on statistical methods and neural networks, constraint-based information extraction systems are still commonly used in industry applications. Chiticariu et al suggest that this might be because constraint-based systems can easily incorporate domain knowledge (2013). The need to incorporate constraints into information extraction systems, as well as the difficulty of doing this efficiently, have been recognized for some time.

Several hybrid approaches combine constraint-based and statistical methods. Toutanova et al model dependencies between semantic frame arguments with a CRF (2008). Chang et al incorporate declarative constraints into statistical sequence-based models to obtain constrained conditional models (2012). When making a prediction (inference step), their model solves an integer linear program. This typically involves maximizing a scoring function, based e.g. on a CRF, over all outputs that satisfy the constraints, resulting in high computational costs. Täckström et al recently proposed a more computationally efficient approach to semantic role labeling with constraints, introducing a dynamic programming approach for inference for log-linear models with constraints (2015).

There are several purely statistical approaches, such as those using hidden Markov models (Baum and Petrie, 1966), CRFs (Lafferty et al., 2001) or structured support vector machines (Tsochantaridis et al., 2004).

Our approach is fundamentally different from all of the above. We propose to boost the precision of an existing information extraction system using a neural network trained with free noisy supervision. Our method does not require large amounts of human annotations as purely statistical or neural network-based approaches would. Our work could also be used to boost the precision of other state-of-the-art constraint or hybrid methods.

2 Design

2.1 Overview

The information extraction pipeline we developed consists of four stages (see right pane "execution" in Figure 2).

1. **Generate candidate extractions**: The document is parsed using a potentially constraint-based or hybrid statistical parser, which outputs a set of candidate extractions. Each candidate extraction consists of the character offsets of all extracted constituent entities, and a representation of the extracted relation. It may additionally contain auxiliary information that the parser may have generated, such as part-of-speech tags.

2. **Score extractions using trained neural network**: Each candidate extraction generated, together with the section of the document it was found in, is encoded into feature data X. A deep neural network is used to compute a neural network correctness score $\tilde{s}$ for each extraction candidate. We detail the input and architecture of the neural network in Section 2.2 and its training in Section 2.3.

3. **Score extractions based on cheap, noisy supervision**: We compute a consistency score s for the candidate extraction, measuring if the extracted relation is consistent with cheaply available, but potentially noisy supervision from e.g. an existing database. We discuss how s is computed in Section 2.4.

4. **Classify extractions as correct or incorrect**: A linear classifier classifies extraction candidates as correct and incorrect extractions, based on neural network correctness score $\tilde{s}$, database consistency score s, and potentially other features. Candidates classified as incorrect are discarded.

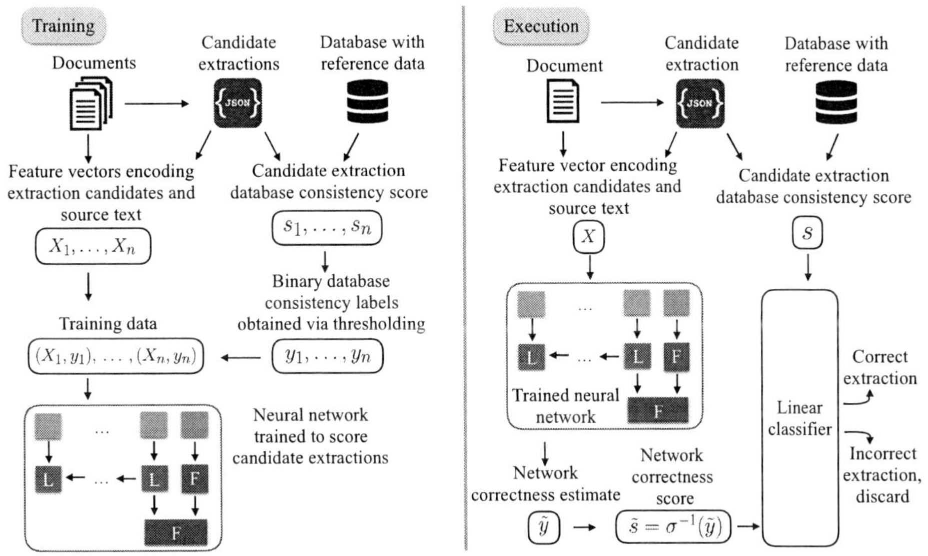

Figure 2: Training (left) and execution (right) set-up. Blocks marked "L" are neural network LSTM cells, while blocks marked "F" are fully-connected layers.

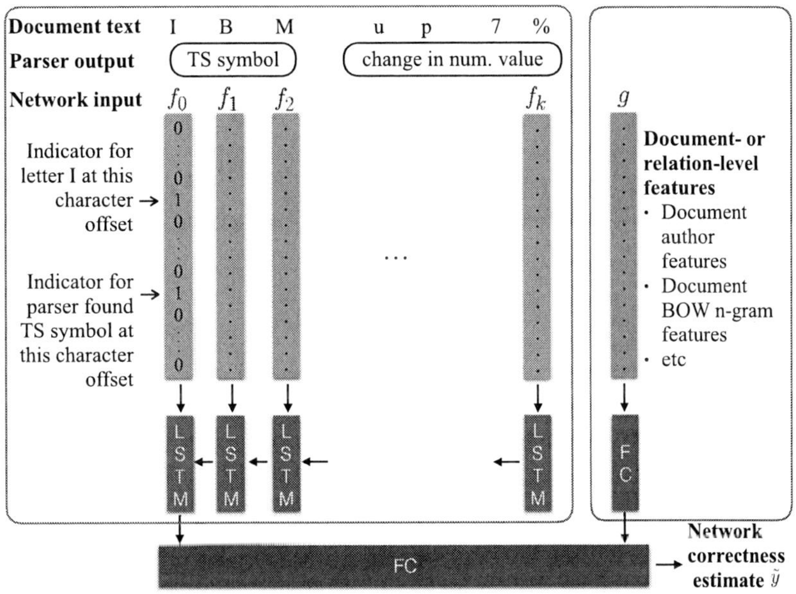

Figure 3: We use a neural network comprised of (i) an LSTM processing encoded parser output and document text character-by-character (labeled LSTM, green), (ii) a fully-connected layer (FC, blue) that takes document-level features as input, and (iii) a fully-connected layer (FC, grey) that takes the output vectors of the layers (i) and (ii) as input to generate a correctness estimate for the extraction candidate. Layer (iii) uses a sigmoid activation function to generate a correctness estimate $\tilde{y} \in (0, 1)$, from which we compute the network correctness score as $\tilde{s} := \sigma^{-1}(\tilde{y})$.

2.2 Neural network input and architecture

The neural network processes each candidate extraction independently. To estimate the correctness of an extracted candidate, the network is provided with two pieces of input (see Figure 3 for the full structure of the neural network). First, the network is provided with a vector g (right box in Figure 3) containing document- or extraction-level features, such as attributes of the document's author, or word-level n-gram features. The second piece of input consists of a sequence of vectors f_i (left box in Figure 3), encoding the document text and the parser's output at the character level. There is one vector f_i for each character c_i of the document section where the extraction candidate is found.

The vectors f_i are a concatenation of (i) a one-hot encoding of the character, and (ii) information about entities the parser identified at the position of c_i. For (i) we use a restricted character set of size 94, including `[a-zA-Z0-9]` and several whitespace, special characters, and an indicator to represent characters not present in our character set. For (ii), we include in f_i a vector of indicators specifying whether or not any of the entities appearing in the relations supported by the parser were found in the position of character c_i.

The input vectors f_i feed into an LSTM, which accumulates state until the input sequence has been exhausted. The global feature vector g feeds into a fully-connected layer, which is then concatenated with the output of the LSTM, and passed through another fully-connected layer with sigmoid activation σ to produce a network correctness estimate $\tilde{y}$. We subsequently compute the network correctness score $\tilde{s}$ for the candidate extraction via $\tilde{s} = \sigma^{-1}(\tilde{y})$.

We regularize the LSTM weight matrices and state vector using dropout (see (Srivastava et al., 2014) and (Zaremba et al., 2015)). Similar to (Sutskever et al., 2014), we found that reversing the LSTM's input resulted in a substantial increase in accuracy.

2.3 Neural network training

We train the neural network by referencing candidates extracted by the high-recall candidate-generating parser against a potentially noisy reference source (see Figure 2, left panel on "training"). In our application, this reference is Bloomberg's proprietary database of historical time series data, which enables us to check how well the extracted numerical data fits into time series in the database. Concretely, we compute a consistency score $s \in (-\infty, \infty)$ that measures the degree of consistency with the database. Depending on the application, the score may for instance be a squared relative error, an absolute error, or a more complex error function. In many applications, the score s will be noisy (see Section 2.4 for further discussion). We threshold s to obtain binary correctness labels $y \in \{0, 1\}$. We then use the binary correctness labels y for supervised neural network training, with binary cross-entropy loss as the loss function. This allows us to train a network that can compute a pseudo-likelihood $\tilde{y} \in (0, 1)$ of a given extraction candidate to agree with the database. Thus, $\tilde{y}$ estimates how likely the extraction candidate is correct.

The neural network's training data consists of candidates generated by the candidate-generating parser, and noisy binary consistency labels y.

In our application, the database labeled a large majority of candidates as correct. To obtain balanced training data, we generated 6 sets of training data, each containing the same set of around 1 million negative cases and disjoint sets of 1 million positive cases each. Correspondingly, we trained an ensemble of 6 networks, and averaged their network scores $\tilde{s}$. We found this to work much better than oversampling the smaller class.

2.4 Noisy supervision

We assume that the noise in the source of supervision is limited in magnitude, e.g. $< 5\%$. We moreover assume that there are no strong patterns in the distribution of the noise: if the noise correlates with certain attributes of the candidate extraction, the pseudo-likelihoods $\tilde{y}$ might no longer be a good estimate of the candidate extraction's probability of being a correct extraction.

There are two sources of noise in our application's database supervision. First, there is a high rate of false positives. It is not rare for the parser to generate an extraction candidate *ts_tick_abs (TS symbol, numerical value)* in which the numerical value fits into the time series of the time series symbol, but the extraction is nonetheless incorrect. False negatives are also a problem: many financial time series are sparse and are rarely observed. As a result, it is common for differences between reference numerical values and extracted numerical values to be large even for correct extractions. Limits for acceptable differences between extracted data and reference data are incorporated into the computation of the database consistency score s. The formula for computing s is application dependent, and may involve auxiliary data related to the extracted entities.

3 Results

Compared to using the existing, highly-tuned, client-facing extraction systems, this work reduced the number of false positive extractions by more than 90%, while the drop in recall was smaller than 1%. Our character-level neural network considerably boosted the precision of the existing information extraction systems, and is being deployed to production.

We are not aware of alternative approaches that can improve an existing extraction engine in a way that is directly comparable to ours. Purely neural network-based or purely statistical approaches require large amounts of human annotation, while our method does not. Constraint-based or hybrid statistical approaches are competitors to the existing extraction system rather than our work; indeed, our work could also be used to boost the precision of state-of-the-art constraint or hybrid methods.

When trained with 256 LSTM hidden units, and 2 million samples for 150 epochs, the neural network alone achieved a training accuracy of 95.8% and a test accuracy of 94.9%, relative to the noisy database supervision. Note that since the supervision provided by the databases is imperfect, it is not unexpected that the network's accuracy is substantially below 100%. We examined the errors in the training set, and found that they are primarily due to the network generalizing correctly, with the network being correct almost always when strongly disagreeing with the database's label.

We include in Figure 4 how data size and network size affect network accuracy. Note that the network's accuracy decreases substantially if the network size (number of LSTM units) is reduced. Accuracy also decreases if smaller quantities of training data are available. To achieve acceptably small latencies in client-serving scenarios, we limit the network size to 256 LSTM hidden units, even though larger networks could achieve slightly greater accuracies. We moreover limited the document input text provided to the LSTM neural network to the lines on which the extraction candidate was found.

Besides the neural network architecture described in this paper, we also considered an approach based on character-level n-grams (see Figure 5). In this approach, we replaced the LSTM

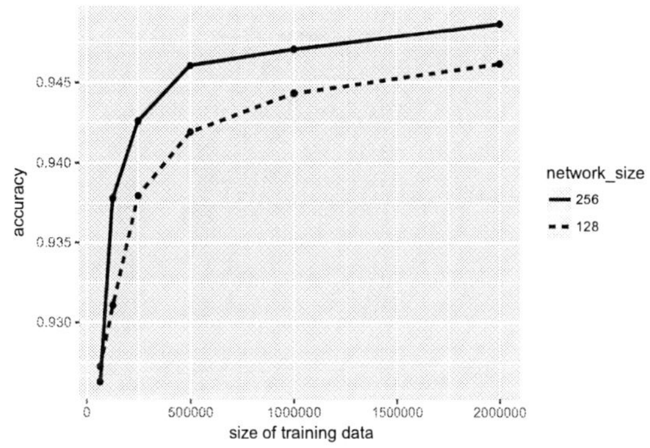

Figure 4: Neural network accuracies for different network and training data sizes.

unit of the neural network with a single fully-connected layer. At the same time, we replaced the character-level input sequence $f_0, \ldots, f_k$ with a single binary vector representing a bag-of-words of n-grams. More precisely, we computed character-level feature vectors $f'_0, \ldots, f'_k$ analogously to the f_i, except that the f'_i contain encodings of character classes (upper case letter, lower case letter, digit, and the same list of special characters used in the f_i) rather than of characters themselves. Each binary vector f'_i was then mapped to a string $\tilde{f'}_i$ containing the same sequence of 0s and 1s as f'_i. Finally, we computed n-grams over the sequence of strings $\tilde{f'}_i$. All n-gram features were tf-idf normalized. We cross-validated on a validation set to tune various hyperparameters, and found that using 2-grams up to 12-grams worked best. The resulting classifier achieve an accuracy of 96.9% on the training set, and 90.4% on the test set. This constitutes a big gap to the 94.9% test accuracy achieved by the neural network, especially since we estimate the accuracy of the database supervision to be around 95%. This suggests that the recurrent neural network was able to internally compute higher-quality features than the bag-of-words n-gram features.

4 Discussion

In this work, we presented an architecture for information extraction from text using a combination of an existing parser and a deep neural network. The deep neural network can boost the precision of an existing high-recall parser. To train the neural network, we use measures of consistency

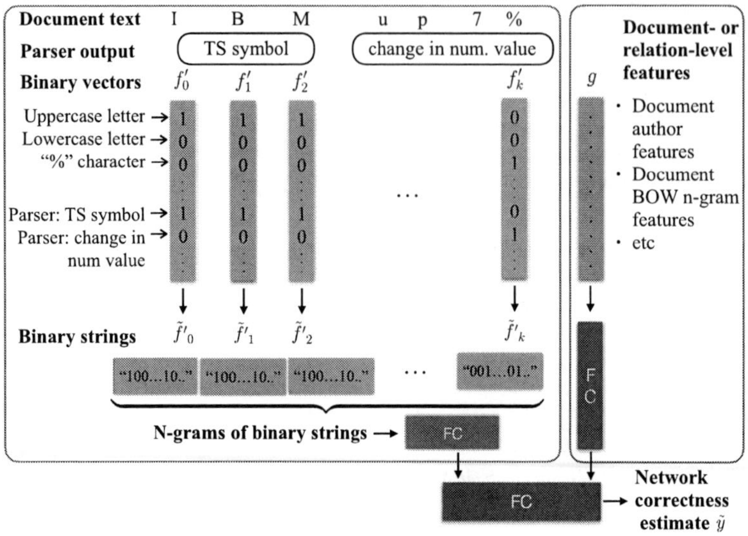

Figure 5: Extraction candidate correctness estimation with an n-gram-based classifier. It differs from Figure 3 only in the green fully connected layer labeled FC, and its input.

between extracted data and existing databases as a form of noisy supervision. The architecture resulted in substantial improvements over mature and highly-tuned information extraction systems for financial language text at Bloomberg. While we used time series databases to derive measures of consistency for candidate extractions, our setup can easily be applied to a variety of other information extraction tasks for which potentially noisy reference data is cheaply available.

We believe our encoding of document text and parser output makes learning particularly easy for the neural network. We encode the candidate-generating parser's document annotations character-by-character into vectors f_i that also include a one-hot encoding of the character itself. We believe that this encoding makes it easier for the network to learn character-level characteristics of the entities that are part of the semantic frame. As an additional benefit, our encoding lends itself well to processing both by recurrent architectures (processing character-by-character input vectors f_i) and convolutional architectures (performing 1D convolutions over an input matrix whose columns are vectors f_i).

Our architecture can easily incorporate global attributes of the document. In our application, we found it useful to add one-hot encoded n-gram and word shape features of the document, allowing the neural network to consider information that might be located far from where the extraction candidate was found. Other potentially useful features could be based on document length, document embeddings, document creator features, and more.

We experimented with other neural network architectures. A slight variation would be to use a bidirectional LSTM instead of a simple LSTM. In addition to LSTM architectures, we experimented with character-level convolutional neural networks. In this setting, we concatenated the vectors f_i into a single matrix for all character indices, and performed 1D convolutions and pooling operations 3 times, and pass the result through a fully-connected layer. We found the performance of this approach to be very similar to that of the LSTM we used. Finally, a hybrid approach, stacking an LSTM on a single convolutional layer, gave very similar results as the LSTM and convolutional architectures.

One could use a variety of sources of information as distant and cheap supervision. While we used existing databases, other applications may use supervision e.g. from user interactions with the extracted data, say if the extracted data is presented to a user who can accept, modify, or reject the extraction. In such a system, the linear classifier classifying candidate extractions would have only a single feature, i.e. the neural network score.

Acknowledgments

We would like to thank my managers Alex Bozic, Tim Phelan, and Joshwini Pereira for supporting this project, as well as David Rosenberg from the CTO's office for providing access to GPU infrastructure.

References

Miguel Ballesteros, Chris Dyer, and A. Noah Smith. 2015. Improved transition-based parsing by modeling characters instead of words with lstms. In *EMNLP*. pages 349–359.

Leonard E. Baum and Ted Petrie. 1966. Statistical inference for probabilistic functions of finite state Markov chains. *Annals of Math. Statistics* .

Ming-Wei Chang, Lev Ratinov, and Dan Roth. 2012. Structured learning with constrained conditional models. *Machine Learning* 88(3):399–431.

Laura Chiticariu, Yunyao Li, and R. Frederick Reiss. 2013. Rule-based information extraction is dead! long live rule-based information extraction systems! In *EMNLP*. pages 827–832.

Jason PC Chiu and Eric Nichols. 2015. Named entity recognition with bidirectional LSTM-CNNs. http://arxiv.org/pdf/1511.08308v4.pdf.

Cicero dos Santos and Maira Gatti. 2014. Deep convolutional neural networks for sentiment analysis of short texts. In *COLING*. pages 69–78.

Felix Gehrs. 2001. *Long Short-Term Memory in Recurrent Neural Networks*. Ph.D. thesis, École polytechnique Fédérale de Lausanne.

Sepp Hochreiter and Jürgen Schmidhuber. 1997. Long short-term memory. *Neural Comput.* 9(8):1735–1780.

Andrej Karpathy. 2015. The unreasonable effectiveness of recurrent neural networks. http://karpathy.github.io/2015/05/21/rnn_effectiveness/.

Yoon Kim. 2014. Convolutional neural networks for sentence classification. In *EMNLP*. pages 1746–1751.

Yoon Kim, Yacine Jernite, David Sontag, and Alexander M. Rush. 2016. Character-aware neural language models. In *AAAI*. pages 2741–2749.

Stefan Kombrink, Tomas Mikolov, Martin Karafiát, and Lukás Burget. 2011. Recurrent neural network based language modeling in meeting recognition. In *INTERSPEECH*.

John D. Lafferty, Andrew McCallum, and Fernando C. N. Pereira. 2001. Conditional random fields: Probabilistic models for segmenting and labeling sequence data. In *ICML*. pages 282–289.

Makoto Miwa and Mohit Bansal. 2016. End-to-end relation extraction using lstms on sequences and tree structures. In *ACL*. Assoc. Comp. Ling., pages 1105–1116.

Huu Thien Nguyen, Kyunghyun Cho, and Ralph Grishman. 2016. Joint event extraction via recurrent neural networks. In *NAACL*. pages 300–309.

Huu Thien Nguyen and Ralph Grishman. 2015. Event detection and domain adaptation with convolutional neural networks. In *ACL*. pages 365–371.

M. Schuster and K. K. Paliwal. 1997. Bidirectional recurrent neural networks. *IEEE Trans. Signal Processing* 45(11):2673–2681.

Richard Socher, John Bauer, D. Christopher Manning, and Ng Andrew Y. 2013. Parsing with compositional vector grammars. In *ACL*. pages 455–465.

Nitish Srivastava, Geoffrey Hinton, Alex Krizhevsky, Ilya Sutskever, and Ruslan Salakhutdinov. 2014. Dropout: A simple way to prevent neural networks from overfitting. *JMLR* 15(1):1929–1958.

Ilya Sutskever, Oriol Vinyals, and Quoc V. Le. 2014. Sequence to sequence learning with neural networks. In *NIPS*. pages 3104–3112.

Oscar Täckström, Kuzman Ganchev, and Dipanjan Das. 2015. Efficient inference and structured learning for semantic role labeling. *Transactions of the Association of Computational Linguistics* 3:29–41.

Kristina Toutanova, Aria Haghighi, and Christopher D. Manning. 2008. A global joint model for semantic role labeling. *Comp. Ling.* 34(2).

Ioannis Tsochantaridis, Thomas Hofmann, Thorsten Joachims, and Yasemin Altun. 2004. Support vector machine learning for interdependent and structured output spaces. In *ICML*. pages 104–.

Wojciech Zaremba, Ilya Sutskever, and Oriol Vinyals. 2015. Recurrent neural network regularization. https://arxiv.org/abs/1409.2329.

Xiang Zhang, Junbo Zhao, and Yann LeCun. 2015. Character-level convolutional networks for text classification. In *NIPS*. pages 649–657.

Jie Zhou and Wei Xu. 2015. End-to-end learning of semantic role labeling using recurrent neural networks. In *ACL*. pages 1127–1137.

Piecewise Latent Variables for Neural Variational Text Processing

Iulian V. Serban[1*] and **Alexander G. Ororbia II**[2*] and **Joelle Pineau**[3] and **Aaron Courville**[1]
[1] Department of Computer Science and Operations Research, Universite de Montreal
[2]College of Information Sciences & Technology, Penn State University
[3]School of Computer Science, McGill University
iulian [DOT] vlad [DOT] serban [AT] umontreal [DOT] ca
ago109 [AT] psu [DOT] edu
jpineau [AT] cs [DOT] mcgill [DOT] ca
aaron [DOT] courville [AT] umontreal [DOT] ca

Abstract

Advances in neural variational inference have facilitated the learning of powerful directed graphical models with continuous latent variables, such as variational autoencoders. The hope is that such models will learn to represent rich, multi-modal latent factors in real-world data, such as natural language text. However, current models often assume simplistic priors on the latent variables — such as the uni-modal Gaussian distribution — which are incapable of representing complex latent factors efficiently. To overcome this restriction, we propose the simple, but highly flexible, piecewise constant distribution. This distribution has the capacity to represent an exponential number of modes of a latent target distribution, while remaining mathematically tractable. Our results demonstrate that incorporating this new latent distribution into different models yields substantial improvements in natural language processing tasks such as document modeling and natural language generation for dialogue.

1 Introduction

The development of the variational autoencoder framework (Kingma and Welling, 2014; Rezende et al., 2014) has paved the way for learning large-scale, directed latent variable models. This has led to significant progress in a diverse set of machine learning applications, ranging from computer vision (Gregor et al., 2015; Larsen et al., 2016) to natural language processing tasks (Mnih and Gregor, 2014; Miao et al., 2016; Bowman et al., 2015; Serban et al., 2017b). It is hoped that this framework will enable the learning of generative processes of real-world data — including text, audio and images — by disentangling and representing the underlying latent factors in the data. However, latent factors in real-world data are often highly complex. For example, topics in newswire text and responses in conversational dialogue often posses latent factors that follow non-linear (non-smooth), multi-modal distributions (i.e. distributions with multiple local maxima).

Nevertheless, the majority of current models assume a simple prior in the form of a multivariate Gaussian distribution in order to maintain mathematical and computational tractability. This is often a highly restrictive and unrealistic assumption to impose on the structure of the latent variables. First, it imposes a strong uni-modal structure on the latent variable space; latent variable samples from the generating model (prior distribution) all cluster around a single mean. Second, it forces the latent variables to follow a perfectly symmetric distribution with constant kurtosis; this makes it difficult to represent asymmetric or rarely occurring factors. Such constraints on the latent variables increase pressure on the down-stream generative model, which in turn is forced to carefully partition the probability mass for each latent factor throughout its intermediate layers. For complex, multi-modal distributions — such as the distribution over topics in a text corpus, or natural language responses in a dialogue system — the uni-modal Gaussian prior inhibits the model's ability to extract and represent important latent structure in the data. In order to learn more expressive latent variable models, we therefore need more flexible, yet tractable, priors.

In this paper, we introduce a simple, flexible

*The first two authors contributed equally.

Proceedings of the 2nd Workshop on Structured Prediction for Natural Language Processing, pages 52–62
Copenhagen, Denmark, September 7–11, 2017.

prior distribution based on the piecewise constant distribution. We derive an analytical, tractable form that is applicable to the variational autoencoder framework and propose a differentiable parametrization for it. We then evaluate the effectiveness of the distribution when utilized both as a prior and as approximate posterior across variational architectures in two natural language processing tasks: document modeling and natural language generation for dialogue. We show that the piecewise constant distribution is able to capture elements of a target distribution that cannot be captured by simpler priors — such as the uni-modal Gaussian. We demonstrate state-of-the-art results on three document modeling tasks, and show improvements on a dialogue natural language generation. Finally, we illustrate qualitatively how the piecewise constant distribution represents multi-modal latent structure in the data.

2 Related Work

The idea of using an artificial neural network to approximate an inference model dates back to the early work of Hinton and colleagues (Hinton and Zemel, 1994; Hinton et al., 1995; Dayan and Hinton, 1996). Researchers later proposed Markov chain Monte Carlo methods (MCMC) (Neal, 1992), which do not scale well and mix slowly, as well as variational approaches which require a tractable, factored distribution to approximate the true posterior distribution (Jordan et al., 1999). Others have since proposed using feed-forward inference models to initialize the mean-field inference algorithm for training Boltzmann architectures (Salakhutdinov and Larochelle, 2010; Ororbia II et al., 2015). Recently, the variational autoencoder framework (VAE) was proposed by Kingma and Welling (2014) and Rezende et al. (2014), closely related to the method proposed by Mnih and Gregor (2014). This framework allows the joint training of an inference network and a directed generative model, maximizing a variational lower-bound on the data log-likelihood and facilitating exact sampling of the variational posterior. Our work extends this framework.

With respect to document modeling, neural architectures have been shown to outperform well-established topic models such as Latent Dirichlet Allocation (LDA) (Hofmann, 1999; Blei et al., 2003). Researchers have successfully proposed several models involving discrete latent variables (Salakhutdinov and Hinton, 2009; Hinton and Salakhutdinov, 2009; Srivastava et al., 2013; Larochelle and Lauly, 2012; Uria et al., 2014; Lauly et al., 2016; Bornschein and Bengio, 2015; Mnih and Gregor, 2014). The success of such discrete latent variable models — which are able to partition probability mass into separate regions — serves as one of our main motivations for investigating models with more flexible continuous latent variables for document modeling. More recently, Miao et al. (2016) proposed to use continuous latent variables for document modeling.

Researchers have also investigated latent variable models for dialogue modeling and dialogue natural language generation (Bangalore et al., 2008; Crook et al., 2009; Zhai and Williams, 2014). The success of discrete latent variable models in this task also motivates our investigation of more flexible continuous latent variables. Closely related to our proposed approach is the Variational Hierarchical Recurrent Encoder-Decoder (*VHRED*, described below) (Serban et al., 2017b), a neural architecture with latent multivariate Gaussian variables.

Researchers have explored more flexible distributions for the latent variables in VAEs, such as autoregressive distributions, hierarchical probabilistic models and approximations based on MCMC sampling (Rezende et al., 2014; Rezende and Mohamed, 2015; Kingma et al., 2016; Ranganath et al., 2016; Maaløe et al., 2016; Salimans et al., 2015; Burda et al., 2016; Chen et al., 2017; Ruiz et al., 2016). These are all complimentary to our approach; it is possible to combine them with the piecewise constant latent variables. In parallel to our work, multiple research groups have also proposed VAEs with discrete latent variables (Maddison et al., 2017; Jang et al., 2017; Rolfe, 2017; Johnson et al., 2016). This is a promising line of research, however these approaches often require approximations which may be inaccurate when applied to larger scale tasks, such as document modeling or natural language generation. Finally, discrete latent variables may be inappropriate for certain natural language processing tasks.

3 Neural Variational Models

We start by introducing the neural variational learning framework. We focus on modeling discrete output variables (e.g. words) in the context of natural language processing applications. However, the framework can easily be adapted to handle continuous output variables.

3.1 Neural Variational Learning

Let $w_1, \ldots, w_N$ be a sequence of N tokens (words) conditioned on a continuous latent variable z. Further, let c be an additional observed variable which conditions both z and $w_1, \ldots, w_N$. Then, the distribution over words is:

$$P_\theta(w_1, \ldots, w_N|c) = \int \prod_{n=1}^{N} P_\theta(w_n|w_{<n}, z, c) P_\theta(z|c) dz,$$

where θ are the model parameters. The model first generates the higher-level, continuous latent variable z conditioned on c. Given z and c, it then generates the word sequence $w_1, \ldots, w_N$. For unsupervised modeling of documents, the c is excluded and the words are assumed to be independent of each other, when conditioned on z:

$$P_\theta(w_1, \ldots, w_N) = \int \prod_{n=1}^{N} P_\theta(w_n|z) P_\theta(z) dz.$$

Model parameters can be learned using the variational lower-bound (Kingma and Welling, 2014):

$$\begin{aligned} &\log P_\theta(w_1, \ldots, w_N|c) \\ &\quad \geq \mathrm{E}_{z \sim Q_\psi(z|w_1,\ldots,w_N,c)}[\log P_\theta(w_n|w_{<n}, z, c)] \\ &\quad - \mathrm{KL}\left[Q_\psi(z|w_1, \ldots, w_N, c)||P_\theta(z|c)\right], \quad (1) \end{aligned}$$

where we note that $Q_\psi(z|w_1, \ldots, w_N, c)$ is the approximation to the intractable, true posterior $P_\theta(z|w_1, \ldots, w_N, c)$. Q is called the *encoder*, or sometimes the *recognition model* or *inference model*, and it is parametrized by ψ. The distribution $P_\theta(z|c)$ is the prior model for z, where the only available information is c. The VAE framework further employs the re-parametrization trick, which allows one to move the derivative of the lower-bound inside the expectation. To accomplish this, z is parametrized as a transformation of a fixed, parameter-free random distribution $z = f_\theta(\epsilon)$, where ϵ is drawn from a random distribution. Here, f is a transformation of ϵ, parametrized by θ, such that $f_\theta(\epsilon) \sim P_\theta(z|c)$. For example, ϵ might be drawn from a standard Gaussian distribution and f might be defined as $f_\theta(\epsilon) = \mu + \sigma\epsilon$, where μ and σ are in the parameter set θ. In this case, z is able to represent any Gaussian with mean μ and variance σ^2.

Model parameters are learned by maximizing the variational lower-bound in eq. (1) using gradient descent, where the expectation is computed using samples from the approximate posterior.

The majority of work on VAEs propose to parametrize z as multivariate Gaussian distribtions. However, this unrealistic assumption may critically hurt the expressiveness of the latent variable model. See Appendix A for a detailed discussion. This motivates the proposed piecewise constant latent variable distribution.

3.2 Piecewise Constant Distribution

We propose to learn latent variables by parametrizing z using a piecewise constant probability density function (PDF). This should allow z to represent complex aspects of the data distribution in latent variable space, such as non-smooth regions of probability mass and multiple modes.

Let $n \in \mathbb{N}$ be the number of piecewise constant components. We assume z is drawn from PDF:

$$P(z) = \frac{1}{K} \sum_{i=1}^{n} 1_{\left(\frac{i-1}{n} \leq z \leq \frac{i}{n}\right)} a_i, \quad (2)$$

where $1_{(x)}$ is the indicator function, which is one when x is true and otherwise zero. The distribution parameters are $a_i > 0$, for $i = 1, \ldots, n$. The normalization constant is:

$$K = \sum_{i=1}^{n} K_i, \text{ where } K_0 = 0, K_i = \frac{a_i}{n}, \text{ for } i = 1, \ldots, n.$$

It is straightforward to show that a piecewise constant distribution with more than $n > 2$ pieces is capable of representing a bi-modal distribution. When $n > 2$, a vector z of piecewise constant variables can represent a probability density with $2^{|z|}$ modes. Figure 1 illustrates how these variables help model complex, multi-modal distributions.

In order to compute the variational bound, we need to draw samples from the piecewise constant distribution using its inverse cumulative distribution function (CDF). Further, we need to compute the KL divergence between the prior and posterior. The inverse CDF and KL divergence quantities are both derived in Appendix B. During training we must compute derivatives of the variational bound in eq. (1). These expressions involve derivatives of indicator functions, which have derivatives zero everywhere except for the changing points where the derivative is undefined. However, the probability of sampling the value exactly at its changing

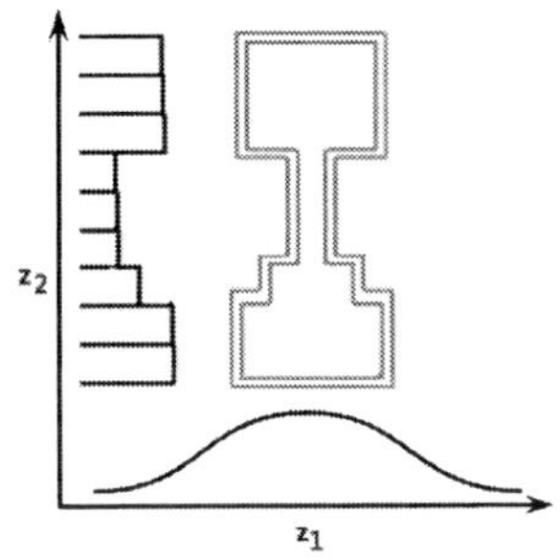

Figure 1: Joint density plot of a pair of Gaussian and piecewise constant variables. The horizontal axis corresponds to z_1, which is a univariate Gaussian variable. The vertical axis corresponds to z_2, which is a piecewise constant variable.

point is effectively zero. Thus, we fix these derivatives to zero. Similar approximations are used in training networks with rectified linear units.

4 Latent Variable Parametrizations

In this section, we develop the parametrization of both the Gaussian variable and our proposed piecewise constant latent variable.

Let x be the current output sequence, which the model must generate (e.g. $w_1, \ldots, w_N$). Let c be the observed conditioning information. If the task contains additional conditioning information this will be embedded by c. For example, for dialogue natural language generation c represents an embedding of the dialogue history, while for document modeling $c = \emptyset$.

4.1 Gaussian Parametrization

Let μ^{prior} and $\sigma^{2,\text{prior}}$ be the prior mean and variance, and let μ^{post} and $\sigma^{2,\text{post}}$ be the approximate posterior mean and variance. For Gaussian latent variables, the prior distribution mean and variances are encoded using linear transformations of a hidden state. In particular, the prior distribution covariance is encoded as a diagonal covariance matrix using a softplus function:

$$\mu^{\text{prior}} = H_\mu^{\text{prior}} \text{Enc}(c) + b_\mu^{\text{prior}},$$
$$\sigma^{2,\text{prior}} = \text{diag}(\log(1 + \exp(H_\sigma^{\text{prior}} \text{Enc}(c) + b_\sigma^{\text{prior}}))),$$

where $\text{Enc}(c)$ is an embedding of the conditioning information c (e.g. for dialogue natural language generation this might, for example, be produced by an LSTM encoder applied to the dialogue history), which is shared across all latent variable dimensions. The matrices $H_\mu^{\text{prior}}, H_\sigma^{\text{prior}}$ and vectors $b_\mu^{\text{prior}}, b_\sigma^{\text{prior}}$ are learnable parameters. For the posterior distribution, previous work has shown it is better to parametrize the posterior distribution as a linear interpolation of the prior distribution mean and variance and a new estimate of the mean and variance based on the observation x (Fraccaro et al., 2016). The interpolation is controlled by a gating mechanism, allowing the model to turn on/off latent dimensions:

$$\mu^{\text{post}} = (1 - \alpha_\mu)\mu^{\text{prior}} + \alpha_\mu \left(H_\mu^{\text{post}} \text{Enc}(c, x) + b_\mu^{\text{post}} \right),$$
$$\sigma^{2,\text{post}} = (1 - \alpha_\sigma)\sigma^{2,\text{prior}} + \alpha_\sigma \text{diag}(\log(1 + \exp(H_\sigma^{\text{post}} \text{Enc}(c, x) + b_\sigma^{\text{post}}))),$$

where $\text{Enc}(c, x)$ is an embedding of both c and x. The matrices $H_\mu^{\text{post}}, H_\sigma^{\text{post}}$ and the vectors $b_\mu^{\text{post}}, b_\sigma^{\text{post}}, \alpha_\mu, \alpha_\sigma$ are parameters to be learned. The interpolation mechanism is controlled by α_μ and α_σ, which are initialized to zero (i.e. initialized such that the posterior is equal to the prior).

4.2 Piecewise Constant Parametrization

We parametrize the piecewise prior parameters using an exponential function applied to a linear transformation of the conditioning information:

$$a_i^{\text{prior}} = \exp(H_{a,i}^{\text{prior}} \text{Enc}(c) + b_{a,i}^{\text{prior}}), \quad i = 1, \ldots, n,$$

where matrix H_a^{prior} and vector b_a^{prior} are learnable. As before, we define the posterior parameters as a function of both c and x:

$$a_i^{\text{post}} = \exp(H_{a,i}^{\text{post}} \text{Enc}(c, x) + b_{a,i}^{\text{post}}), \quad i = 1, \ldots, n,$$

where H_a^{post} and b_a^{post} are parameters.

5 Variational Text Modeling

We now introduce two classes of VAEs. The models are extended by incorporating the Gaussian and piecewise latent variable parametrizations.

5.1 Document Model

The neural variational document model (*NVDM*) model has previously been proposed for document modeling (Mnih and Gregor, 2014; Miao et al., 2016), where the latent variables are Gaussian. Since the original *NVDM* uses Gaussian latent variables, we will refer to it as *G-NVDM*. We propose two novel models building on *G-NVDM*. The first model we propose uses piecewise constant latent variables instead of Gaussian latent variables.

We refer to this model as *P-NVDM*. The second model we propose uses a combination of Gaussian and piecewise constant latent variables. The models sample the Gaussian and piecewise constant latent variables independently and then concatenates them together into one vector. We refer to this model as *H-NVDM*.

Let V be the vocabulary of document words. Let W represent a document matrix, where row w_i is the 1-of-$|V|$ binary encoding of the i'th word in the document. Each model has an encoder component $Enc(W)$, which compresses a document vector into a continuous distributed representation upon which the approximate posterior is built. For document modeling, word order information is not taken into account and no additional conditioning information is available. Therefore, each model uses a bag-of-words encoder, defined as a multi-layer perceptron (MLP) $Enc(c = \emptyset, x) = Enc(x)$. Based on preliminary experiments, we choose the encoder to be a two-layered MLP with parametrized rectified linear activation functions (we omit these parameters for simplicity). For the approximate posterior, each model has the parameter matrix W_a^{post} and vector b_a^{post} for the piecewise latent variables, and the parameter matrices $W_\mu^{\text{post}}, W_\sigma^{\text{post}}$ and vectors $b_\mu^{\text{post}}, b_\sigma^{\text{post}}$ for the Gaussian means and variances. For the prior, each model has parameter vector b_a^{prior} for the piecewise latent variables, and vectors $b_\mu^{\text{prior}}, b_\sigma^{\text{prior}}$ for the Gaussian means and variances. We initialize the bias parameters to zero in order to start with centered Gaussian and piecewise constant priors. The encoder will adapt these priors as learning progresses, using the gating mechanism to turn on/off latent dimensions.

Let z be the vector of latent variables sampled according to the approximate posterior distribution. Given z, the decoder $Dec(w, z)$ outputs a distribution over words in the document:

$$Dec(w, z) = \frac{\exp\left(-w^{\mathrm{T}}Rz + b_w\right)}{\sum_{w'} \exp\left(-w^{\mathrm{T}}Rz + b_{w'}\right)},$$

where R is a parameter matrix and b is a parameter vector corresponding to the bias for each word to be learned. This output probability distribution is combined with the KL divergences to compute the lower-bound in eq. (1). See Appendix C.

Our baseline model *G-NVDM* is an improvement over the original *NVDM* proposed by Mnih and Gregor (2014) and Miao et al. (2016). We learn the prior mean and variance, while these were fixed to a standard Gaussian in previous work. This increases the flexibility of the model and makes optimization easier. In addition, we use a gating mechanism for the approximate posterior of the Gaussian variables. This gating mechanism allows the model to turn off latent variable (i.e. fix the approximate posterior to equal the prior for specific latent variables) when computing the final posterior parameters. Furthermore, Miao et al. (2016) alternated between optimizing the approximate posterior parameters and the generative model parameters, while we optimize all parameters simultaneously.

5.2 Dialogue Model

The variational hierarchical recurrent encoder-decoder (*VHRED*) model has previously been proposed for dialogue modeling and natural language generation (Serban et al., 2017b, 2016a). The model decomposes dialogues using a two-level hierarchy: sequences of utterances (e.g. sentences), and sub-sequences of tokens (e.g. words). Let $\mathbf{w}_n$ be the n'th utterance in a dialogue with N utterances. Let $w_{n,m}$ be the m'th word in the n'th utterance from vocabulary V given as a 1-of-$|V|$ binary encoding. Let M_n be the number of words in the n'th utterance. For each utterance $n = 1, \ldots, N$, the model generates a latent variable z_n. Conditioned on this latent variable, the model then generates the next utterance:

$$P_\theta(\mathbf{w}_1, z_1, \ldots, \mathbf{w}_N, z_N) = \prod_{n=1}^{N} P_\theta(z_n|\mathbf{w}_{<n}) \times \prod_{m=1}^{M_n} P_\theta(w_{n,m}|w_{n,<m}, \mathbf{w}_{<n}, z_n),$$

where θ are the model parameters. *VHRED* consists of three RNN modules: an *encoder* RNN, a *context* RNN and a *decoder* RNN. The *encoder* RNN computes an embedding for each utterance. This embedding is fed into the *context* RNN, which computes a hidden state summarizing the dialogue context before utterance n: h_{n-1}^{con}. This state represents the additional conditioning information, which is used to compute the prior distribution over z_n:

$$P_\theta(z_n \mid \mathbf{w}_{<n}) = f_\theta^{\text{prior}}(z_n; h_{n-1}^{con}),$$

where f^{prior} is a PDF parametrized by both θ and h_{n-1}^{con}. A sample is drawn from this distribution: $z_n \sim P_\theta(z_n|\mathbf{w}_{<n})$. This sample is given as input

to the *decoder* RNN, which then computes the output probabilities of the words in the next utterance. The model is trained by maximizing the variational lower-bound, which factorizes into independent terms for each sub-sequence (utterance):

$$\log P_\theta(\mathbf{w}_1, \ldots, \mathbf{w}_N)$$
$$\geq \sum_{n=1}^{N} - \mathrm{KL}\left[Q_\psi(z_n \mid \mathbf{w}_1, \ldots, \mathbf{w}_n) || P_\theta(z_n \mid \mathbf{w}_{<n})\right]$$
$$+ \mathbb{E}_{Q_\psi(z_n|\mathbf{w}_1,\ldots,\mathbf{w}_n)}\left[\log P_\theta(\mathbf{w}_n \mid z_n, \mathbf{w}_{<n})\right],$$

where distribution Q_ψ is the approximate posterior distribution with parameters ψ, computed similarly as the prior distribution but further conditioned on the *encoder* RNN hidden state of the next utterance.

The original *VHRED* model (Serban et al., 2017b) used Gaussian latent variables. We refer to this model as *G-VHRED*. The first model we propose uses piecewise constant latent variables instead of Gaussian latent variables. We refer to this model as *P-VHRED*. The second model we propose takes advantage of the representation power of both Gaussian and piecewise constant latent variables. This model samples both a Gaussian latent variable z_n^{gaussian} and a piecewise latent variable $z_n^{\text{piecewise}}$ independently conditioned on the *context* RNN hidden state:

$$P_\theta(z_n^{\text{gaussian}} \mid \mathbf{w}_{<n}) = f_\theta^{\text{prior, gaussian}}(z_n^{\text{gaussian}}; h_{n-1}^{con}),$$
$$P_\theta(z_n^{\text{piecewise}} \mid \mathbf{w}_{<n}) = f_\theta^{\text{prior, piecewise}}(z_n^{\text{piecewise}}; h_{n-1}^{con}),$$

where $f^{\text{prior, gaussian}}$ and $f^{\text{prior, piecewise}}$ are PDFs parametrized by independent subsets of parameters θ. We refer to this model as *H-VHRED*.

6 Experiments

We evaluate the proposed models on two types of natural language processing tasks: document modeling and dialogue natural language generation. All models are trained with back-propagation using the variational lower-bound on the log-likelihood or the exact log-likelihood. We use the first-order gradient descent optimizer Adam (Kingma and Ba, 2015) with gradient clipping (Pascanu et al., 2012)[1]

Model	20-NG	RCV1	CADE
LDA	1058	−−	−−
docNADE	896	−−	−−
NVDM	836	−−	−−
G-NVDM	651	905	339
H-NVDM-3	607	865	**258**
H-NVDM-5	**566**	**833**	294

Table 1: Test perplexities on three document modeling tasks: 20-NewGroup (20-NG), Reuters corpus (RCV1) and CADE12 (CADE). Perplexities were calculated using 10 samples to estimate the variational lower-bound. The *H-NVDM* models perform best across all three datasets.

6.1 Document Modeling

Tasks We use three different datasets for document modeling experiments. First, we use the 20 News-Groups (20-NG) dataset (Hinton and Salakhutdinov, 2009). Second, we use the Reuters corpus (RCV1-V2), using a version that contained a selected 5,000 term vocabulary. As in previous work (Hinton and Salakhutdinov, 2009; Larochelle and Lauly, 2012), we transform the original word frequencies using the equation $\log(1 + \text{TF})$, where TF is the original word frequency. Third, to test our document models on text from a non-English language, we use the Brazilian Portuguese CADE12 dataset (Cardoso-Cachopo, 2007). For all datasets, we track the validation bound on a subset of 100 vectors randomly drawn from each training corpus.

Training All models were trained using mini-batches with 100 examples each. A learning rate of 0.002 was used. Model selection and early stopping were conducted using the validation lower-bound, estimated using five stochastic samples per validation example. Inference networks used 100 units in each hidden layer for 20-NG and CADE, and 100 for RCV1. We experimented with both 50 and 100 latent random variables for each class of models, and found that 50 latent variables performed best on the validation set. For *H-NVDM* we vary the number of components used in the PDF, investigating the effect that 3 and 5 pieces had on the final quality of the model. The number

[1]Code and scripts are available at https://github.com/aqo109/piecewise-nvdm-emnlp-2017 and https://github.com/julianser/hred-latent-piecewise.

G-NVDM	H-NVDM-3	H-NVDM-5
environment	project	science
project	gov	built
flight	major	high
lab	based	technology
mission	earth	world
launch	include	form
field	science	scale
working	nasa	sun
build	systems	special
gov	technical	area

Table 2: Word query similarity test on 20 News-Groups: for the query 'space", we retrieve the top 10 nearest words in word embedding space based on Euclidean distance. *H-NVDM-5* associates multiple meanings to the query, while *G-NVDM* only associates the most frequent meaning.

of hidden units was chosen via preliminary experimentation with smaller models. On 20-NG, we use the same set-up as (Hinton and Salakhutdinov, 2009) and therefore report the perplexities of a topic model (*LDA*, (Hinton and Salakhutdinov, 2009)), the document neural auto-regressive estimator (*docNADE*, (Larochelle and Lauly, 2012)), and a neural variational document model with a fixed standard Gaussian prior (*NVDM*, lowest reported perplexity, (Miao et al., 2016)).

Results In Table 1, we report the test document perplexity: $\exp(-\frac{1}{D}\sum_n \frac{1}{L_n} \log P_\theta(x_n)$. We use the variational lower-bound as an approximation based on 10 samples, as was done in (Mnih and Gregor, 2014). First, we note that the best baseline model (i.e. the *NVDM*) is more competitive when both the prior and posterior models are learnt together (i.e. the *G-NVDM*), as opposed to the fixed prior of (Miao et al., 2016). Next, we observe that integrating our proposed piecewise variables yields even better results in our document modeling experiments, substantially improving over the baselines. More importantly, in the 20-NG and Reuters datasets, increasing the number of pieces from 3 to 5 further reduces perplexity. Thus, we have achieved a new state-of-the-art perplexity on 20 News-Groups task and — to the best of our knowledge – better perplexities on the CADE12 and RCV1 tasks compared to using a state-of-the-art model like the *G-NVDM*. We also evaluated the converged models using an non-parametric inference procedure, where a separate approximate posterior is learned for each test example in order to tighten the variational lower-bound. *H-NVDM* also performed best in this evaluation across all three datasets, which confirms that the performance improvement is due to the piecewise components. See appendix for details.

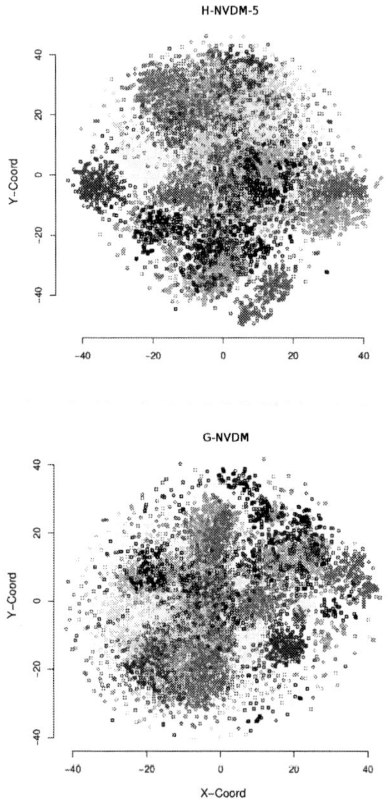

Figure 2: Latent variable approximate posterior means t-SNE visualization on 20-NG for *G-NVDM* and *H-NVDM-5*. Colors correspond to the topic labels assigned to each document.

In Table 2, we examine the top ten highest ranked words given the query term "space", using the decoder parameter matrix. The piecewise variables appear to have a significant effect on what is uncovered by the model.In the case of "space", the hybrid with 5 pieces seems to value two senses of the word–one related to "outer space" (e.g., "sun", "world", etc.) and another related to the dimensions of depth, height, and width within which things may exist and move (e.g., "area", "form", "scale", etc.). On the other hand, *G-NVDM* appears to only capture the "outer space" sense of

Model	Activity	Entity
HRED	4.77	2.43
G-VHRED	**9.24**	2.49
P-VHRED	5	2.49
H-VHRED	8.41	**3.72**

Table 3: Ubuntu evaluation using F1 metrics w.r.t. activities and entities. *G-VHRED*, *P-VHRED* and *H-VHRED* all outperform the baseline *HRED*. *G-VHRED* performs best w.r.t. activities and *H-VHRED* performs best w.r.t. entities.

the word. More examples are in the appendix.

Finally, we visualized the means of the approximate posterior latent variables on 20-NG through a t-SNE projection. As shown in Figure 2, both *G-NVDM* and *H-NVDM-5* learn representations which disentangle the topic clusters on 20-NG. However, *G-NVDM* appears to have more dispersed clusters and more outliers (i.e. data points in the periphery) compared to *H-NVDM-5*. Although it is difficult to draw conclusions based on these plots, these findings could potentially be explained by the Gaussian latent variables fitting the latent factors poorly.

6.2 Dialogue Modeling

Task We evaluate *VHRED* on a natural language generation task, where the goal is to generate responses in a dialogue. This is a difficult problem, which has been extensively studied in the recent literature (Ritter et al., 2011; Lowe et al., 2015; Sordoni et al., 2015; Li et al., 2016; Serban et al., 2016a,b). Dialogue response generation has recently gained a significant amount of attention from industry, with high-profile projects such as Google SmartReply (Kannan et al., 2016) and Microsoft Xiaoice (Markoff and Mozur, 2015). Even more recently, Amazon has announced the Alexa Prize Challenge for the research community with the goal of developing a natural and engaging chatbot system (Farber, 2016).

We evaluate on the technical support response generation task for the Ubuntu operating system. We use the well-known Ubuntu Dialogue Corpus (Lowe et al., 2015, 2017), which consists of about 1/2 million natural language dialogues extracted from the #Ubuntu Internet Relayed Chat (IRC) channel. The technical problems discussed span a wide range of software-related and hardware-related issues. Given a dialogue history — such as a conversation between a user and a technical support assistant — the model must generate the next appropriate response in the dialogue. For example, when it is the turn of the technical support assistant, the model must generate an appropriate response helping the user resolve their problem.

We evaluate the models using the activity- and entity-based metrics designed specifically for the Ubuntu domain (Serban et al., 2017a). These metrics compare the *activities* and *entities* in the model generated responses with those of the reference responses; activities are verbs referring to high-level actions (e.g. *download*, *install*, *unzip*) and entities are nouns referring to technical objects (e.g. *Firefox*, *GNOME*). The more activities and entities a model response overlaps with the reference response (e.g. expert response) the more likely the response will lead to a solution.

Training The models were trained to maximize the log-likelihood of training examples using a learning rate of 0.0002 and mini-batches of size 80. We use a variant of truncated back-propagation. We terminate the training procedure for each model using early stopping, estimated using one stochastic sample per validation example. We evaluate the models by generating dialogue responses: conditioned on a dialogue context, we fix the model latent variables to their median values and then generate the response using a beam search with size 5. We select model hyper-parameters based on the validation set using the F1 activity metric, as described earlier.

It is often difficult to train generative models for language with stochastic latent variables (Bowman et al., 2015; Serban et al., 2017b). For the latent variable models, we therefore experiment with reweighing the KL divergence terms in the variational lower-bound with values 0.25, 0.50, 0.75 and 1.0. In addition to this, we linearly increase the KL divergence weights starting from zero to their final value over the first 75000 training batches. Finally, we weaken the *decoder* RNN by randomly replacing words inputted to the decoder RNN with the unknown token with 25% probability. These steps are important for effectively training the models, and the latter two have been used in previous work by Bowman et al. (2015) and Serban et al. (2017b).

HRED (Baseline): We compare to the *HRED* model (Serban et al., 2016a): a sequence-to-sequence model, shown to outperform other established models on this task, such as the LSTM RNN language model (Serban et al., 2017a). The *HRED* model's *encoder* RNN uses a bidirectional GRU RNN encoder, where the forward and backward RNNs each have 1000 hidden units. The context RNN is a GRU encoder with 1000 hidden units, and the decoder RNN is an LSTM decoder with 2000 hidden units.[2] The encoder and context RNNs both use layer normalization (Ba et al., 2016).[3] We also experiment with an additional rectified linear layer applied on the inputs to the decoder RNN. As with other hyper-parameters, we choose whether to include this additional layer based on the validation set performance. *HRED*, as well as all other models, use a word embedding dimensionality of size 400.

G-HRED: We compare to *G-VHRED*, which is *VHRED* with Gaussian latent variables (Serban et al., 2017b). *G-VHRED* uses the same hyper-parameters for the encoder, context and decoder RNNs as the HRED model. The model has 100 Gaussian latent variables per utterance.

P-HRED: The first model we propose is *P-VHRED*, which is *VHRED* model with piecewise constant latent variables. We use $n = 3$ number of pieces for each latent variable. *P-VHRED* also uses the same hyper parameters for the encoder, context and decoder RNNs as the *HRED* model. Similar to *G-VHRED*, *P-VHRED* has 100 piecewise constant latent variables per utterance.

H-HRED: The second model we propose is *H-VHRED*, which has 100 piecewise constant (with $n = 3$ pieces per variable) and 100 Gaussian latent variables per utterance. *H-VHRED* also uses the same hyper-parameters for the encoder, context and decoder RNNs as *HRED*.

Results: The results are given in Table 3. All latent variable models outperform *HRED* w.r.t. both activities and entities. This strongly suggests that the high-level concepts represented by the latent variables help generate meaningful, goal-directed responses. Furthermore, each type of latent variable appears to help with a different aspects of the generation task. *G-VHRED* performs best w.r.t. activities (e.g. *download*, *install* and so on), which occur frequently in the dataset. This suggests that the Gaussian latent variables learn useful latent representations for frequent actions. On the other hand, *H-VHRED* performs best w.r.t. entities (e.g. *Firefox*, *GNOME*), which are often much rarer and mutually exclusive in the dataset. This suggests that the combination of Gaussian and piecewise latent variables help learn useful representations for entities, which could not be learned by Gaussian latent variables alone. We further conducted a qualitative analysis of the model responses, which supports these conclusions. See Appendix G.[4]

7 Conclusions

In this paper, we have sought to learn rich and flexible multi-modal representations of latent variables for complex natural language processing tasks. We have proposed the piecewise constant distribution for the variational autoencoder framework. We have derived closed-form expressions for the necessary quantities required for in the autoencoder framework, and proposed an efficient, differentiable implementation of it. We have incorporated the proposed piecewise constant distribution into two model classes — *NVDM* and *VHRED* — and evaluated the proposed models on document modeling and dialogue modeling tasks. We have achieved state-of-the-art results on three document modeling tasks, and have demonstrated substantial improvements on a dialogue modeling task. Overall, the results highlight the benefits of incorporating the flexible, multi-modal piecewise constant distribution into variational autoencoders. Future work should explore other natural language processing tasks, where the data is likely to arise from complex, multi-modal latent factors.

Acknowledgments

The authors acknowledge NSERC, Canada Research Chairs, CIFAR, IBM Research, Nuance Foundation and Microsoft Maluuba for funding. Alexander G. Ororbia II was funded by a NACME-Sloan scholarship. The authors thank Hugo Larochelle for sharing the NewsGroup 20 dataset. The authors thank Laurent Charlin, Sungjin Ahn, and Ryan Lowe for constructive feedback. This research was enabled in part by support provided by Calcul Qubec (`www.calculquebec.ca`) and Compute Canada (`www.computecanada.ca`).

[2]Since training lasted between 1-3 weeks for each model, we had to fix the number of hidden units during preliminary experiments on the training and validation datasets.

[3]We did not apply layer normalization to the decoder RNN, because several of our colleagues have found that this may hurt the performance of generative language models.

[4]Results on a Twitter dataset are given in the appendix.

References

J. L. Ba, J. R. Kiros, and G. E. Hinton. 2016. Layer normalization. *arXiv preprint arXiv:1607.06450*.

S. Bangalore, G. Di Fabbrizio, and A. Stent. 2008. Learning the structure of task-driven human–human dialogs. *IEEE Transactions on Audio, Speech, and Language Processing*, 16(7):1249–1259.

D. M. Blei, A. Y. Ng, and M. I. Jordan. 2003. Latent dirichlet allocation. *JAIR*, 3:993–1022.

J. Bornschein and Y. Bengio. 2015. Reweighted wake-sleep. In *ICLR*.

S. R. Bowman, L. Vilnis, O. Vinyals, A. M. Dai, R. Jozefowicz, and S. Bengio. 2015. Generating sentences from a continuous space. In *Conference on Computational Natural Language Learning*.

Y. Burda, R. Grosse, and R. Salakhutdinov. 2016. Importance weighted autoencoders. *ICLR*.

A. Cardoso-Cachopo. 2007. Improving Methods for Single-label Text Categorization. PdD Thesis, Instituto Superior Tecnico, Universidade Tecnica de Lisboa.

X. Chen, D. P. Kingma, T. Salimans, Y. Duan, P. Dhariwal, J. Schulman, I. Sutskever, and P. Abbeel. 2017. Variational lossy autoencoder. In *ICLR*.

N. Crook, R. Granell, and S. Pulman. 2009. Unsupervised classification of dialogue acts using a dirichlet process mixture model. In *Special Interest Group on Discourse and Dialogue (SIGDIAL)*, pages 341–348.

P. Dayan and G. E. Hinton. 1996. Varieties of helmholtz machine. *Neural Networks*, 9(8):1385–1403.

L. Devroye. 1986. Sample-based non-uniform random variate generation. In *Proceedings of the 18th conference on Winter simulation*, pages 260–265. ACM.

M. Farber. 2016. Amazon's 'Alexa Prize' Will Give College Students Up To $2.5M To Create A Socialbot. *Fortune*.

M. Fraccaro, S. K. Sønderby, U. Paquet, and O. Winther. 2016. Sequential neural models with stochastic layers. In *NIPS*, pages 2199–2207.

K. Gregor, I. Danihelka, A. Graves, and D. Wierstra. 2015. DRAW: A recurrent neural network for image generation. In *ICLR*.

G. E. Hinton, P. Dayan, B. J. Frey, and R. M. Neal. 1995. The" wake-sleep" algorithm for unsupervised neural networks. *Science*, 268(5214):1158–1161.

G. E. Hinton and R. Salakhutdinov. 2009. Replicated softmax: an undirected topic model. In *NIPS*, pages 1607–1614.

G. E. Hinton and R. S. Zemel. 1994. Autoencoders, minimum description length and helmholtz free energy. In *NIPS*, pages 3–10. NIPS.

T. Hofmann. 1999. Probabilistic latent semantic indexing. In *ACM SIGIR Conference on Research and Development in Information Retrieval*, pages 50–57. ACM.

E. Jang, S. Gu, and B. Poole. 2017. Categorical reparameterization with gumbel-softmax. In *ICLR*.

M. Johnson, D. K. Duvenaud, A. Wiltschko, R. P. Adams, and S. R. Datta. 2016. Composing graphical models with neural networks for structured representations and fast inference. In *NIPS*, pages 2946–2954.

M. I. Jordan, Z. Ghahramani, T. S. Jaakkola, and L. K. Saul. 1999. An introduction to variational methods for graphical models. *Machine Learning*, 37(2):183–233.

A. Kannan, K. Kurach, et al. 2016. Smart Reply: Automated Response Suggestion for Email. In *KDD*.

D. Kingma and J. Ba. 2015. Adam: A method for stochastic optimization. In *ICLR*.

D. P. Kingma, T. Salimans, and M. Welling. 2016. Improving variational inference with inverse autoregressive flow. *NIPS*, pages 4736–4744.

D. P. Kingma and M. Welling. 2014. Auto-encoding variational Bayes. *ICLR*.

H. Larochelle and S. Lauly. 2012. A neural autoregressive topic model. In *NIPS*, pages 2708–2716.

A. B. Lindbo Larsen, S. K. Sønderby, and O. Winther. 2016. Autoencoding beyond pixels using a learned similarity metric. In *ICML*, pages 1558–1566.

S. Lauly, Y. Zheng, A. Allauzen, and H. Larochelle. 2016. Document neural autoregressive distribution estimation. *arXiv preprint arXiv:1603.05962*.

J. Li, M. Galley, C. Brockett, J. Gao, and B. Dolan. 2016. A diversity-promoting objective function for neural conversation models. In *The North American Chapter of the Association for Computational Linguistics (NAACL)*, pages 110–119.

Ryan Lowe, Nissan Pow, Iulian Serban, and Joelle Pineau. 2015. The Ubuntu Dialogue Corpus: A Large Dataset for Research in Unstructured Multi-Turn Dialogue Systems. In *Special Interest Group on Discourse and Dialogue (SIGDIAL)*.

Ryan T. Lowe, Nissan Pow, Iulian V. Serban, Laurent Charlin, Chia-Wei Liu, and Joelle Pineau. 2017. Training End-to-End Dialogue Systems with the Ubuntu Dialogue Corpus. *Dialogue & Discourse*, 8(1).

Lars Maaløe, Casper Kaae Sønderby, Søren Kaae Sønderby, and Ole Winther. 2016. Auxiliary deep generative models. In *ICML*, pages 1445–1453.

C. J. Maddison, A. Mnih, and Y. W. Teh. 2017. The concrete distribution: A continuous relaxation of discrete random variables. In *ICLR*.

J. Markoff and P. Mozur. 2015. For Sympathetic Ear, More Chinese Turn to Smartphone Program. *New York Times*.

Y. Miao, L. Yu, and P. Blunsom. 2016. Neural variational inference for text processing. In *ICML*, pages 1727–1736.

A. Mnih and K. Gregor. 2014. Neural variational inference and learning in belief networks. In *ICML*, pages 1791–1799.

R. M. Neal. 1992. Connectionist learning of belief networks. *Artificial intelligence*, 56(1):71–113.

A. G. Ororbia II, C. L. Giles, and D. Reitter. 2015. Online semi-supervised learning with deep hybrid boltzmann machines and denoising autoencoders. *arXiv preprint arXiv:1511.06964*.

R. Pascanu, T. Mikolov, and Y. Bengio. 2012. On the difficulty of training recurrent neural networks. *ICML*, 28:1310–1318.

Rajesh Ranganath, Dustin Tran, and David Blei. 2016. Hierarchical variational models. In *ICML*, pages 324–333.

D. J. Rezende and S. Mohamed. 2015. Variational inference with normalizing flows. In *ICML*, pages 1530–1538.

D. J. Rezende, S. Mohamed, and D. Wierstra. 2014. Stochastic backpropagation and approximate inference in deep generative models. In *ICML*, pages 1278–1286.

A. Ritter, C. Cherry, and W. B. Dolan. 2011. Data-driven response generation in social media. In *Proceedings of the Conference on Empirical Methods in Natural Language Processing*, pages 583–593.

J. T. Rolfe. 2017. Discrete variational autoencoders. In *ICLR*.

Francisco R Ruiz, Michalis Titsias RC AUEB, and David Blei. 2016. The generalized reparameterization gradient. In *NIPS*, pages 460–468.

R. Salakhutdinov and G. E. Hinton. 2009. Semantic hashing. *International Journal of Approximate Reasoning*, 50(7):969–978.

R. Salakhutdinov and H. Larochelle. 2010. Efficient learning of deep boltzmann machines. In *AISTATs*, pages 693–700.

T. Salimans, D. P Kingma, and M. Welling. 2015. Markov chain monte carlo and variational inference: Bridging the gap. In *ICML*, pages 1218–1226.

R. Sennrich, B. Haddow, and A. Birch. 2016. Neural machine translation of rare words with subword units. In *Association for Computational Linguistics (ACL)*.

I. V. Serban, T. Klinger, G. Tesauro, K. Talamadupula, B. Zhou, Y. Bengio, and A. Courville. 2017a. Multiresolution recurrent neural networks: An application to dialogue response generation. In *Thirty-First AAAI Conference (AAAI)*.

I. V. Serban, A. Sordoni, Y. Bengio, A. Courville, and J. Pineau. 2016a. Building end-to-end dialogue systems using generative hierarchical neural network models. In *Thirtieth AAAI Conference (AAAI)*.

I. V. Serban, A. Sordoni, R. Lowe, L. Charlin, J. Pineau, A. Courville, and Y. Bengio. 2017b. A hierarchical latent variable encoder-decoder model for generating dialogues. In *Thirty-First AAAI Conference (AAAI)*.

Iulian Vlad Serban, Ryan Lowe, Laurent Charlin, and Joelle Pineau. 2016b. Generative deep neural networks for dialogue: A short review. In *NIPS, Let's Discuss: Learning Methods for Dialogue Workshop*.

A. Sordoni, M. Galley, M. Auli, C. Brockett, Y. Ji, M. Mitchell, J. Nie, J. Gao, and B. Dolan. 2015. A neural network approach to context-sensitive generation of conversational responses. In *Conference of the North American Chapter of the Association for Computational Linguistics (NAACL-HLT 2015)*, pages 196–205.

N. Srivastava, R. R Salakhutdinov, and G. E. Hinton. 2013. Modeling documents with deep boltzmann machines. In *Proceedings of the Twenty-Ninth Conference on Uncertainty in Artificial Intelligence (UAI)*, pages 616–624.

B. Uria, I. Murray, and H. Larochelle. 2014. A deep and tractable density estimator. In *ICML*, pages 467–475.

K. Zhai and J. D. Williams. 2014. Discovering latent structure in task-oriented dialogues. In *Association for Computational Linguistics (ACL)*, pages 36–46.

Author Index

Association for Computational Linguistics
209 N. Eighth Street
Stroudsburg, Pennsylvania 18360

ISBN 978-1-5108-4751-4

9 781510 847514

CURRAN ASSOCIATES INC.
proceedings.com